Contents

Capelet Swing Cardi

MATERIALS

Yarn

RED HEART® *Eco-Ways™*, 4oz/113g skeins, each approx 186yd/170m (acrylic/recycled polyester)
• 7 (9, 10) skeins #3313 Oyster

Hook
• Size H/8 (5mm) crochet hook *or size to obtain gauge*

Notions
• 2 buttons—1⅜"/35mm diameter (for outer buttons)
• 1 button—1"/25mm diameter (for inner button)
• Stitch markers
• Yarn needle

SIZES
S/M (L/1X, 2X/3X)

FINISHED MEASUREMENTS
Chest/waist 37 (46, 53)"/94 (117, 134.5)cm
Length 36"/91.5cm
Note Coat fits a large range of sizes. Snuggest part of coat fits below bust (high waist). Fit is customized by overlapping front edges and placing buttons carefully. S/M will fit busts approx 34–40"/86.5–101.5cm, L/1X will fit busts approx 42–50"/106.5–127cm, 2X/3X will fit busts approx 50–56"/127–142cm.

GAUGE
7 (sc, dc) repeats and 11½ rows = 4"/10cm over (sc, dc) pattern using size H/8 (5mm) crochet hook.
Remember to check gauge for best results!

NOTES
1 This design can be worked in a variety of styles: coat, long jacket, short jacket, or capelet only. The capelet is worked first from the center front edges around using "short rows" to form the curved shape. Then the body is worked downward, and it can be tried on while working to desired length.

2 To make a long jacket (about 28"/71cm long), you will need one less ball of yarn. To make a short jacket (about 22"/56cm long), you will need two fewer balls of yarn. To make the capelet only you will need three fewer balls of yarn.

CAPELET
Beginning at one center front edge, ch 56.
Row 1 (wrong side) (Sc, dc) in 2nd ch from hook, *sk next ch, (sc, dc) in next ch; repeat from * across—28 (sc, dc) pattern repeats.
Rows 2–22 Ch 1, turn, (sc, dc) in first st, *sk next st, (sc, dc) in next st; repeat from * across.

Begin "Short Row" Shaping
Short Row 1 (right side) Ch 1, turn; (sc, dc) in first st, [sk next st, (sc, dc) in next st] 6 times; leave remaining sts unworked—7 (sc, dc) pattern repeats.
Short Row 2 Ch 1, turn; (sc, dc) in first st, *sk next st, (sc, dc) in next st; repeat from * across.
Short Row 3 Ch 1, turn; (sc, dc) in first st, *sk next st, (sc, dc) in next st; repeat from * across; working in unworked st of previous row [sk next st, (sc, dc) in next st] 7 times; leave remaining sts unworked—14 (sc, dc) pattern repeats.
Short Rows 4 and 5 Repeat Short Rows 2 and 3—21 (sc, dc) pattern repeats.
Short Row 6 Repeat Short Row 2.
Short Row 7 Ch 1, turn; (sc, dc) in first st, *sk next st, (sc, dc) in next st; repeat from * across; working in unworked st of previous row [sk next st, (sc, dc) in next st] 6 times; leave remaining sts unworked—27 (sc, dc) pattern repeats.
Short Row 8 Repeat Short Row 2.
Short Row 9 Ch 1, turn; (sc, dc) in first st, *sk next st, (sc, dc) in next st; repeat from * across; working in unworked sts of previous row, sk next st, (sc, dc) in next st—28 (sc, dc) pattern repeats.
Short Rows 10–12 Ch 1, turn; (sc, dc) in first st, *sk next st, (sc, dc) in next st; repeat from * across.
Short Rows 13–132 (168, 192) Repeat last 12 short rows 10 (13, 15) more times.

Next 19 Rows Ch 1, turn; (sc, dc) in first st, *sk next st, (sc, dc) in next st; repeat from * across.
Last Row Ch 1, turn; (sc, dc) in first st, [sk next st, (sc, dc) in next st] 11 times, ch 9, sk next st, sc in next st, place a marker in sc just made; working along ch-9 just made, sc in each ch across (buttonloop made), dc in marked sc, *sk next st, (sc, dc) in next st; repeat from * across. Fasten off.
Note This completes the capelet. The shorter of the two long edges forms the neck edge. The longer of the two long edges forms the lower edge.

BODY
Notice that the long edges of the capelet (ends of rows) appear "scalloped." There should be 87 (105, 117) scallops along the lower edge of the capelet.
Row 1 With right side of capelet facing and working in scallops along lower edge, join yarn with sc in first scallop, [ch 2, sc in next scallop] 15 (19, 23) times, ch 15, sk next 18 (19, 19) scallops (for armhole), sc in next scallop, [ch 2, sc in next scallop] 18 (26, 30) times, ch 15, sk next 18 (19, 19) scallops (for armhole), sc in next scallop, [ch 2, sc in next scallop] 15 (19, 23) times—51 (67, 79) sc, 48 (64, 76) ch-2 sps, and 2 ch-15 sps.
Row 2 (wrong side) Ch 1, turn; **(sc, dc) in next sc, *sk next ch-2 sp, (sc, dc) in next sc; repeat from * across to armhole ch-15 sp, sk first ch, [(sc, dc) in next ch, sk next ch] 7 times; repeat from ** once more, (sc, dc) in next sc, ***sk next ch-2 sp, (sc, dc) in next sc; repeat from *** across—65 (81, 93) (sc, dc) pattern repeats.
Rows 3–14 Ch 1, turn; (sc, dc) in first st, *sk next st, (sc, dc) in next st; repeat from * across.
Row 15 (increase row—right side) Ch 1, turn; (sc, dc) in first st, [sk next st, (sc, dc) in next st] 19 (25, 29) times, do not sk next st, (sc, dc) in next 2 sts (increase made), place a marker in 2nd to last dc just made, [sk next st, (sc, dc) in next st] 11 (13, 15) times, do not sk next st, (sc, dc) in next 2 sts (increase made), place a marker in last dc just made, [sk next st, (sc, dc) in next

Capelet Swing Cardi

next 2 sts] 3 times, **sk next st, (sc, dc) in next st; repeat from ** across—71 (87, 99) (sc, dc) pattern repeats.

Rows 20–55 Repeat last 4 rows 9 more times—98 (114, 126) (sc, dc) pattern repeats.

Rows 56–58 Ch 1, turn; (sc, dc) in first st, *sk next st, (sc, dc) in next st; repeat from * across.

Row 59 Ch 1, turn; (sc, hdc, dc) in first st, *sk next st, sl st in next st, sk next st, (sc, hdc, dc) in next st; repeat from * across. Fasten off.

FINISHING

Button Loops

Make two button loops for outer buttons with one at the right front waist edge (where capelet meets body) and another at right front capelet edge 4"/10cm below top edge as follows:

Loop Row Join yarn with sc in edge, ch 9, sc in same sp as first sc, turn, working along ch-9 just made, sc in each ch across (button loop made), sl st in first sc. Fasten off.

Work another button loop, in same manner, on left front edge of capelet, 4"/10cm below top edge (for inner button). Try on coat and place markers on coat to correspond to button loops (one each for button loop at right front edge, left front edge, and waist). Sew buttons at marked locations.

Back Neck

To stabilize back neck, place a marker on each side of the center 5"/12.5cm at back neck, 3"/7.5cm below top edge. Working from wrong side around posts of sts at center back neck, work 14 sc evenly spaced between the markers. Ch 1, turn; sc in each of the 14 sc across. Fasten off. Weave in all ends. ■

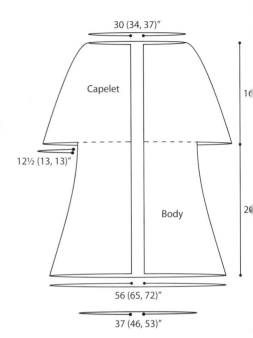

st] 11 (13, 15) times, do not sk next st, (sc, dc) in next 2 sts (increase made), place a marker in last dc just made, [sk next st, (sc, dc) in next st] 20 (26, 30) times—68 (84, 96) (sc, dc) pattern repeats.

Note Move markers up as work progresses. When working even rows (not increasing), always move the marker to the dc of the (sc, dc) worked into the marked st. To help keep the increases nicely spaced, when moving a marker into an increase, move the marker to the 2nd to last dc just made in the first increase, the last dc just made in the 3rd increase, and alternate this placement in the middle increase (i.e., place the marker in the 2nd to last dc just made in every other increase row, and in the last dc just made in the other increase rows).

Rows 16–18 Ch 1, turn; (sc, dc) in first st, *sk next st, (sc, dc) in next st; repeat from * across.

Row 19 (increase row—right side) Ch 1, turn; (sc, dc) in next sc, [*sk next st, (sc, dc) in next st; repeat from * across to next marked st, do not sk next st, (sc, dc) in

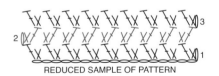

REDUCED SAMPLE OF PATTERN

REDUCED SAMPLE OF SHORT ROWS

Favorite Cardi

MATERIALS

Yarn  3

RED HEART® *Designer Sport*, 3oz/85g skeins, each approx 279yd/255m (acrylic)
- 3 (4, 5) skeins #3515 Lagoon (A)
- 1 skein #3620 Celadon (B)
- 1 skein #3650 Pistachio (C)

Hook
- Size I/9 (5.5mm) crochet hook *or size to obtain gauge*

Notions
- 3 large buttons—1¼"/32mm
- 3 large snap closures
- Yarn needle

SIZES

S (M, L, 1X, 2X, 3X)

FINISHED MEASUREMENTS

Bust 34 (38, 42, 46, 50, 54)"/86.5 (96.5, 106.5, 116.5, 127, 137)cm, including 2"/5cm front band
Length 23 (25, 27, 27, 28, 28)"/58.5 (63.5, 68.5, 68.5, 71, 71)cm

GAUGE

12 sts and 16 rows = 4"/10cm over Griddle Stitch Pattern.
Remember to check gauge for best results!

NOTES

1 Body of cardigan is worked in three pieces; a lower body piece (skirt), an upper body piece (bodice), and a band. The band is sewn between the lower and upper body pieces, to provide strength and shaping.

2 The cardigan is worked in Griddle Stitch. When instructed to work in pattern, always work an sc in each dc and a dc in each sc of previous row.

GRIDDLE STITCH PATTERN

Row 1 Ch 1, turn, *sc in next dc, dc in next sc; repeat from * across.
Repeat Row 1 for Griddle Stitch Pattern.

LOWER BODY

With A, ch 97 (109, 121, 133, 145, 157)
Row 1 Sc in 2nd ch from hook and in each rem ch across—96 (108, 120, 132, 144, 156) sc.
Work in Griddle Stitch Pattern until piece measures 3 (3½, 4, 4, 4, 4)"/7.5 (9, 10, 10, 10, 10)cm from beginning.

Next Row (dec row) Ch 1, turn, [sc in next dc, dc in next sc] 10 (12, 14, 16, 18, 20) times; [sc2tog] twice; [sc in next dc, dc in next sc] 24 (26, 28, 30, 32, 34) times; [sc2tog] twice; [sc in next dc, dc in next sc] 10 (12, 14, 16, 18, 20) times—92 (104, 116, 128, 140, 152) sts.
Continue in Griddle Stitch Pattern until piece measures 6 (7, 8, 8, 8, 8)"/15 (18, 20.5, 20.5, 20.5, 20.5)cm from beginning.
Next Row (dec row) Ch 1, turn, sc in next dc, [dc in next sc, sc in next dc] 9 (11, 13, 15, 17, 19) times, [sc2tog] twice, [dc in next

Favorite Cardi

sc, sc in next dc] 23 (25, 27, 29, 31, 33) times, [sc2tog] twice, dc in next sc, [sc in next dc, dc in next sc] 9 (11, 13, 15, 17, 19) times—88 (100, 112, 124, 136, 148) sts. Continue in Griddle Stitch Pattern until piece measures 9 (10½, 12, 12, 12, 12)"/23 (26.5, 30.5, 30.5, 30.5, 30.5)cm from beginning.

Next Row (dec row) Ch 1, turn, [sc in next dc, dc in next sc] 9 (11, 13, 15, 17, 19) times; [sc2tog] twice; [sc in next dc, dc in next sc] 22 (24, 26, 28, 30, 32) times; [sc2tog] twice; [sc in next dc, dc in next sc] 9 (11, 13, 15, 17, 19) times—84 (96, 108, 120, 132, 144) sts.

Continue in Griddle Stitch Pattern until piece measures 11 (12, 13, 13, 14, 14)"/28 (30.5, 33, 33, 35.5, 35.5)cm from beginning. Fasten off.

UPPER BODY

With A, ch 85 (97, 109, 121, 133, 145).

Row 1 Sc in 2nd ch from hook and in each rem ch across—84 (96, 108, 120, 132, 144) sc.

Rows 2 and 3 Work 2 rows in Griddle Stitch Pattern.

Row 4 (inc row) Ch 1, turn, sc in next dc, [dc in next sc, sc in next dc] 8 (10, 12, 14, 16, 18) times, (dc, sc) in next 2 sts, [dc in next sc, sc in next dc] 23 (25, 27, 29, 31, 33) times, (dc, sc) in next 2 sts, dc in next sc, [sc in next dc, dc in next sc] 8 (10, 12, 14, 16, 18) times—88 (100, 112, 124, 136, 148) sts. Continue in Griddle Stitch Pattern until piece measures 1¾"/4.5cm from beginning.

Row 5 (inc row) Ch 1, turn, [sc in next dc, dc in next sc] 9 (11, 13, 15, 17, 19) times; (sc, dc) in next 2 sts; [sc in next dc, dc in next sc] 24 (26, 28, 30, 32, 34) times; (sc, dc) in next 2 sts; [sc in next dc, dc in next sc] 9 (11, 13, 15, 17, 19) times—92 (104, 116, 128, 140, 152) sts.

Continue in Griddle Stitch Pattern until piece measures 2¾"/7cm from beginning.

Row 6 (inc row) Ch 1, turn, sc in next dc, [dc in next sc, sc in next dc] 9 (11, 13, 15, 17, 19) times, (dc, sc) in next 2 sts, [dc in next sc, sc in next dc] 25 (27, 29, 31, 33, 35) times, (dc, sc) in next 2 sts, dc in next sc, [sc in next dc, dc in next sc] 9 (11, 13, 15, 17, 19) times—96 (108, 120, 132, 144, 156) sts.

Continue in Griddle Stitch Pattern until piece measures 3 (3½, 4, 4, 4, 4)"/7.5 (9, 10, 10, 10, 10)cm from beginning. Do not fasten off.

Right Front

Row 1 (right side) Ch 1, turn, [sc in next dc, dc in next sc] 9 (11, 13, 14, 15, 16) times; leave rem sts unworked (for back and left front)—18 (22, 26, 28, 30, 32) sts. Work in Griddle Stitch Pattern until piece measures 7½ (8, 8½, 8¾, 8½, 8½)"/19 (20.5, 21.5, 21.5, 21.5, 21.5)cm from beginning. End with a right side row.

Shape Neck

Row 1 (wrong side – dec row) Ch 1, turn, work in Griddle Stitch (sc in each dc, dc in each sc) over first 15 (18, 22, 24, 26, 28) sts; leave rem sts unworked—15 (18, 22, 24, 26, 28) sts.

Row 2 (right side – dec row) Ch 1, turn, sc2tog, continue in Griddle Stitch across—14 (17, 21, 23, 25, 27) sts.

Row 3 (dec row) Ch 1, turn, work in Griddle Stitch across to last 2 sts, sc2tog—13 (16, 20, 22, 24, 26) sts.

Rows 4–5 (6, 7, 9, 9, 11) Repeat Rows 2 and 3, 1 (1, 2, 3, 3, 4) times, then repeat Row 2, 0 (1, 0, 0, 0, 0) more time(s)—11 (13, 16, 16, 18, 18) sts.

Work in Griddle Stitch Pattern until piece measures 10½ (11½, 12½, 12½, 12½, 12½)"/26.5 (29, 32, 32, 32, 32)cm. Fasten off.

Back

With right side facing, sk next 6 (6, 6, 8, 10, 12) unworked sts following right front, join A with sl st in next dc.

Row 1 Ch 1, sc in same dc as join, dc in next sc, [sc in next dc, dc in next sc] 23 (25, 27, 29, 31, 33) times; leave rem sts unworked (for left front)—48 (52, 56, 60, 64, 68) sts.

Work in Griddle Stitch Pattern until back measures same as right front. Fasten off.

Left Front

With right side facing, sk next 6 (6, 6, 8, 10, 12) unworked sts following back, join A with sl st in next dc.

Row 1 Ch 1, sc in same dc as join, dc in next sc, *sc in next dc, dc in next sc; repeat from * across—18 (22, 26, 28, 30, 32) sts.

Work in Griddle Stitch Pattern until piece measures 7½ (8, 8½, 8½, 8½, 8½)"/19 (20.5, 21.5, 21.5, 21.5, 21.5)cm from beginning. End with a right side row.

Shape Neck

Row 1 (wrong side – dec row) Ch 1, turn, sl st in first 3 (4, 4, 4, 4, 4) sts, continue in Griddle Stitch across—15 (18, 22, 24, 26, 28) sts (excluding sl sts).

Row 2 (right side – dec row) Ch 1, turn, work in Griddle Stitch across to last 2 sts (excluding sl sts), sc2tog; leave sl sts unworked—14 (17, 21, 23, 25, 27) sts.

Row 3 (dec row) Ch 1, turn, sc2tog, continue in Griddle Stitch across—13 (16, 20, 22, 24, 26) sts.

Rows 4–5 (6, 7, 9, 9, 11) Repeat Rows 2 and 3, 1 (1, 2, 3, 3, 4) times, then repeat Row 2, 0 (1, 0, 0, 0, 0) more time(s)—11 (13, 16, 16, 18, 18) sts.

Work in Griddle Stitch Pattern until piece measures same as back. Fasten off.

BAND

With A, ch 7.

Row 1 Sc in 2nd ch from hook and in each rem ch across—6 sc.

Work in Griddle Stitch Pattern until piece measures 28 (32, 36, 40, 44, 48)"/71 (81.5, 91.5, 101.5, 112, 122)cm from beginning. Fasten off.

SLEEVE (MAKE 2)

With B, ch 43 (47, 51, 51, 55, 55).

Row 1 Sc in 2nd ch from hook and in each rem ch across—42 (46, 50, 50, 54, 54) sc.

Rows 2–4 Work in 3 rows in Griddle Stitch Pattern.

Row 5 (dec row) Ch 1, turn, work in Griddle Stitch over first 5 (6, 7, 7, 8, 8) sts, sc2tog, *continue in Griddle Stitch over next 8 (9, 10, 10, 11, 11) sts, sc2tog; repeat from * 2 more times; continue in Griddle Stitch over rem sts—38 (42, 46, 46, 50, 50) sts.

Continue in Griddle Stitch Pattern until piece measures 2"/5cm from beginning.

FINISHING

Working from wrong side of pieces, sew one long edge of band to top edge of lower body. Sew opposite long edge of band to lower edge of upper body. Sew shoulder seams. Aligning center of sleeve with shoulder seam, sew sleeve in place, easing shoulder as needed, and sewing 1 (1, 1, 1¼, 1¾, 2)"/2.5 (2.5, 2.5, 3, 4.5. 5)cm of sleeve side to each underarm.

Neck Trim
With right side facing, join A with sl st in corner of neck, ch 1, work sc evenly spaced around neck edge to opposite corner. Fasten off.

Front Bands
With right side facing, join C with sl st in lower corner of front edge, ch 1, work sc evenly spaced across front edge (be sure that you have an even number of sts). Work in Griddle Stitch Pattern until band measures 2"/5cm. Fasten off. Repeat on opposite front edge. Sew button along right front band, as follows: sew first but-

ton at top of front band; sew rem two buttons, spaced approx 4"/10cm apart below the first button. Sew one half of a snap closure behind each button. Sew the other half of a snap closure along left front band opposite buttons.
Weave in all ends. ▪

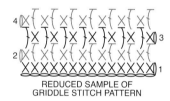

REDUCED SAMPLE OF
GRIDDLE STITCH PATTERN

Next Row (dec row) Ch 1, turn, work in Griddle Stitch over first 3 (4, 4, 4, 5, 5) sts, sc2tog, *continue in Griddle Stitch over the next 7 (8, 9, 9, 10, 10) sts, sc2tog; repeat from * 2 more times; continue in Griddle Stitch over rem sts—32 (38, 42, 42, 46, 46) sts.

Continue in Griddle Stitch Pattern until piece measures 2½"/6.5cm from beginning. Fasten off B. Turn work and join A with sl st in first st.

Continue in Griddle Stitch Pattern until piece measures 3½"/9cm from beginning.
Next Row (inc row) Ch 1, turn, working in Griddle Stitch, work 2 sts in first st (inc made), continue in Griddle Stitch across to last st, work 2 sts in last st—34 (40, 44, 44, 48, 48) sts.
Next 3 Rows Work 3 rows in Griddle Stitch Pattern.
Repeat last 4 rows 4 more times—42 (48, 52, 52, 56, 56) sts.
Continue in Griddle Stitch Pattern until piece measures 10½ (11, 12, 12, 12, 12)"/26.5 (28, 30.5, 30.5, 30.5, 30.5)cm from beginning. Fasten off.

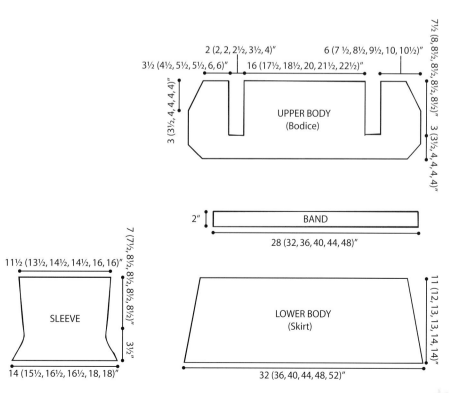

7½ (8, 8½, 8½, 8½, 8½)"

2 (2, 2, 2½, 3½, 4)"

6 (7 ½, 8½, 9½, 10, 10½)"

3½ (4½, 5½, 5½, 6, 6)"

16 (17½, 18½, 20, 21½, 22½)"

3 (3½, 4, 4, 4, 4)"

UPPER BODY
(Bodice)

3 (3½, 4, 4, 4, 4)"

2"

BAND

28 (32, 36, 40, 44, 48)"

11½ (13½, 14½, 14½, 16, 16)"

7 (7½, 8½, 8½, 8½, 8½)"

3½"

SLEEVE

14 (15½, 16½, 16½, 18, 18)"

11 (12, 13, 13, 14, 14)"

LOWER BODY
(Skirt)

32 (36, 40, 44, 48, 52)"

Winter Lace Cardi

MATERIALS

Yarn

RED HEART® *Soft Yarn*, 5oz/140g skeins, each approx 256yd/234m (acrylic)
- 5 (8) skeins in #4601 Off White

Hook
- Size G/6 (4mm) crochet hook *or size to obtain gauge*

Notions
- Yarn needle
- Ivory Ribbon, 2¼ (2¼)yds/206 (228.5)cm

SIZES
S/M (LG/XL)

FINISHED MEASUREMENTS
Chest Approx 39 (48)"/99 (122)cm

GAUGE
27 sts and 15 rows over pattern stitch with G/6 (4mm) crochet hook = 5¾x4¾"(14.5 x12cm).
Remember to check gauge for best results!

PATTERN STITCH
Note Ch 2 at beginning of rows counts as first sc.

Row 1 Ch 2, sk 3 ch, sc in each of next 2 ch, *ch 3, sk 3 chs, sc in next ch, ch 3, sk 1 ch, sc in next ch, ch 3, sk 3 chs, sc in each of next 3 chs. Repeat from * across. Turn.

Row 2 Ch 2, sk first st, sc in each of next 2 sc, *ch 3, sk ch-3 sp, 7 dc in next ch-3 sp, ch 3, sc in each of next 3 sc. Repeat from * across, ending pat with last sc in top of turning ch. Turn.

Row 3 Ch 2, sk first st, sc in next sc, *ch 3, sc in each of next 7 dc, ch 3, sk next sc, sc in next sc. Repeat from * ending pat with sc in last sc, sc in top of turning ch. Turn.

Row 4 Ch 5 (counts as sc, ch 3), sk next ch-3 space, sc in each of next 7 sc, *ch 7, sk next (ch-3, sc, ch-3), sc in each of next

7 sc. Repeat from * across, ending pat with ch 3, sc in top of turning ch. Turn.

Row 5 Ch 5, sc in ch-3 space, ch 3, sk next sc, sc in each of next 5 sc, *(ch 3, sc in ch-7 sp) 2x, ch 3, sk next sc, sc in each of next 5 sc. Repeat from * across, ending pat with ch 3, sc in last ch-5 space, ch 3, sc in same ch-5 space. Turn.

Row 6 Ch 4 (counts as dc), 3 dc in ch-3 sp, *ch 3, sk next ch-3 sp, sk 1 sc, sc in each of next 3 sc, ch 3, sk ch-3 sp, 7 dc in next ch-3 sp. Repeat from * across, ending pat with 4 dc in next ch-5 sp. Turn.

Row 7 Ch 2, skip first dc, sc in each of next 3 dc, *ch 3, sk ch-3 space, sk first sc, sc in next sc, ch 3, sk ch-3 sp, sc in each of next 7 dc. Repeat from * across, ending with sc in each of last 3 dc and top of turning ch. Turn.

Row 8 Ch 2, sk first sc, sc in each of next 3 sc, *ch 7, sk (ch-3, sc, ch-3) sc in each of next 7 sc. Repeat from * across, ending pat with sc in each of next 3 sc and top of turning ch.

Row 9 Ch 2, sk first sc, sc in each of next 2 sc, *(ch 3, sc in ch-7 sp,) 2x, ch 3, sk next sc, sc in each of next 5 sc. Repeat from * across, ending with sc in each of last 2 sc and top of turning ch. Turn.

Row 10 Ch 2, sk first sc, sc in next sc, *ch 3, sk ch-3 sp, 7 dc in next ch-3 sp, ch 3, sk next ch-3 sp, sk next sc, sc in each of next 3 sc. Repeat from * across, ending pat with sk first sc, sc in next sc, sc in top of turning ch. Turn.

Row 11 Ch 5, sk next ch-3 space, sc in each of next 7 dc, *ch 3, sk 1 sc, sc in next sc, ch 3, sc in each of next 7 dc. Repeat from * across, ending pat with ch 3, sc in top of turning ch. Turn.

Row 12 Ch 5, sk next ch-3 space, sc in each of next 7 sc, *ch 7, sk (ch-3, sc, ch-3), sc in each of next 7 sc. Repeat from * across, ending pat with ch 3, sc in last ch-5 sp. Turn.

Row 13 Ch 5, sc in ch-3 space, ch 3, sk next sc, sc in each of next 5 sc, *(ch 3, sc in ch-7 sp) 2x, ch 3, sk next sc, sc in each of next 5 sc. Repeat from * across, ending pat with ch 3, sc in last ch-5 space, ch 3, sc in same ch-5 space. Turn.

Row 14 Ch 4, 3 dc in first ch-3 sp, *ch 3, sk next ch-3 sp, sk next sc, sc in each of next 3 sc, ch 3, sk next ch-3 sp, 7 dc in next ch-3 sp. Repeat from * across, ending 4 dc in last ch-3 sp. Turn.

Row 15 Ch 2, sk first dc, sc in each of next 3 dc, *ch 3, sk next sc, sc in next sc, ch 3, sc in each of next 7 dc. Repeat from * across, ending dc in each of next 3 dc and top of turning ch.
Repeat rows 8–15 for pattern stitch.

NOTES
1 Changes in width will be in ( ) in the directions. Changes in length will be noted in the directions where the rows will be added.
2 This sweater is fitted around the bust, shoulders, and upper arms. It is loose around the hips.

BACK (ODD ROWS ARE RIGHT SIDE)
Note Back is worked on 7 (9) repeats.
Ch 87 (111) + 2.
Rows 1–23 Work rows 1–15 in pat once, then work rows 8–15 in pattern once. Turn.

LG/XL Only

Work rows 8–15 in pat once more.
Row 24 Ch 2, sc in each of the next 2 sc, ch 7, sk (ch-3, sc, ch-3), sc in each of the next 7 sc, continue in pat, ending ch 7, sk (ch-3, sc, ch-3), sc in each of the next 3 sc. Turn.

Row 25 Ch 2, sc in next sc, ch 3, (sc in ch-7 sp, ch 3) 2x, sk 1 sc, sc in next 5 sc, continue in pat, ending ch 3, (sc in ch-7 sp, ch 3) 2x, sk 1 sc, sc in next 2 sc. Turn.

Row 26 Ch 4, sk next ch-3 sp, 7 dc in next ch-3 sp, continue in pat, ending sk next ch-3 sp, 7 dc in next ch-3 sp, ch 3, sc in turning ch. Turn.

Row 27 Ch 4, sc in each of the next 7 dc, continue in pat, ending sc in each of the next 7 dc, ch 2, sc in turning ch. Turn.

Row 28 Ch 2, sc in each of the next 7 sc, continue in pat, ending sc in each of the next 7 sc. Turn.

Row 29 Ch 3, sk first sc, sc in each of the next 5 sc, continue in pat, ending sc in each of the next 5 sc, ch 3, sc in turning ch. Turn.

Winter Lace Cardi

Row 30 Ch 4, dc in first sc, ch 3, sk 1 sc, sc in each of next 3 sc, continue in pat, ending sk 1 sc, sc in each of next 3 sc, ch 3, sc in top of turning ch. Turn.

Row 31 Ch 5, sk next sc, sc in next sc, continue in pat, ending sk next sc, sc in next sc, ch 3, sc in next dc, sc in top of turning ch. Turn.

Row 32 Ch 7, sk (ch-3, sc, ch-3), sc in each of next 7 sc, continue in pat, ending sk (ch-3, sc, ch-3), sc in next sc. Turn.

Row 33 Ch 2, (sc in ch-7 sp, ch 3) 2x, sk next sc, sc in each of next 5 sc, continue in pat, ending (ch-3, sc in ch-7 sp) 2x. Turn.

Row 34 Ch 4, 7 dc in first ch-3 sp, ch 3, sk (sc, ch-3, sc), sc in next 3 sc, continue in pat, ending ch 3, sk ch-3 sp, 7 dc in next ch-3 sp, ch 1, sc in top of turning ch. Turn.

Row 35 Ch 2, sc in each of next 7 dc, continue in pat, ending sc in each of last 7 dc. Turn.

Row 36 Ch 2, sk first sc, sc in each of next 6 sc, ch 7, continue in pat, ending sc in each of next 7 sc. Turn.

Row 37 Ch 2, sk first sc, sc in each of next 5 sc, ch 3, (sc in ch-7 sp, ch 3) 2x, continue in pat, ending sk first sc, sc in each of next 5 sc. Turn.

Row 38 Ch 4, sk first sc, sc in each of next 3 sc, continue in pat, ending sk first sc, sc in each of next 3 sc, ch 2, sc in top of turning ch. Turn.

Row 39 Ch 3, sk 2 sc, sc in next sc, continue in pat, ending sk 1 sc, sc in next sc, ch 3, sc in top of turning ch. Turn.

Rows 40–56 Repeat rows 32–39 two more times. Then repeat row 32 one more time. Turn.

Ribbon Row

Row 57 Ch 4, (dc in ch-7 sp, ch 1) 2x, dc in next sc, *(ch 1, sk 1 sc, dc in next sc) 3x, (ch 1, dc in ch-7 sp) 3x. Repeat from * across, ending (ch1, dc in last 7 sp) 3x. Turn.

UPPER BACK AND SHOULDER

Row 58 Ch 2, sc in first ch-1 sp, ch 3, sc in next ch-1 sp, ch 3, sk 1 ch-1 sp, sc in next ch-1 sp, (sc in next dc, sc in next ch-1 sp) 2x, *ch 3, sk 1 ch-1 sp, sc in next ch-1 sp, ch 3, sc in next ch-1 sp, ch 3, sk 1 ch-1 sp,

sc in next ch-1 sp, (sc in next dc, sc in next ch-1 sp) 2x, repeat from * across, ending with ch 3, sk 1 ch-1 sp, sc in next ch-4 sp, sc in same ch-4 sp. Turn.

Rows 59–63 Repeat rows 35–39.

Rows 64–92 Repeat rows 32–39 three times, then rows 32–36 once.

LG/XL Only
Repeat rows 32–39 one more time. Fasten off.

LEFT FRONT

Note Left Front is worked on 4 (5) repeats. Ch 51 (63) + 2.

Rows 1–23 Work rows 1-15 in pat once, then work rows 8-15 in pattern once. Turn.

LG/XL Only
Work rows 8-15 in pat stitch once more.

Row 24 Continue in established pat, ending ch 7, sk (ch-3, sc, ch-3), sc in each of the next 3 sc. Turn.

Row 25 Ch 2, sc in next sc, ch 3, (sc in ch-7 sp, ch 3) 2x, sk 1 sc, sc in next 5 sc, continue in pat. Turn.

Row 26 Continue in pat, ending sk next ch-3 sp, 7 dc in next ch-3 sp, ch 3, sc in turning ch. Turn.

Row 27 Ch 4, sc in each of the next 7 dc, continue in pat. Turn.

Row 28 Continue in pat, ending sc in each of the next 7 sc. Turn.

Row 29 Ch 3, sk first sc, sc in each of the next 5 sc, continue in pat. Turn.

Row 30 Continue in pat, ending sk 1 sc, sc in each of next 3 sc, ch 3, sc in top of turning ch. Turn.

Row 31 Ch 5, sk next sc, sc in next sc, continue in pat. Turn.

Row 32 Continue in pat, ending sk (ch-3, sc, ch-3), sc in next sc. Turn.

Row 33 Ch 2, (sc in ch-7 sp, ch 3) 2x, sk next sc, sc in each of next 5 sc, continue in pat. Turn.

Row 34 Continue in pat, ending ch 3, sk ch-3 sp, 7 dc in next ch-3 sp, ch 1, sc in top of turning ch. Turn.

Row 35 Ch 2, sc in each of next 7 dc, continue in pat. Turn.

Row 36 Continue in pat, ending sc in each of next 7 sc. Turn.

Row 37 Ch 2, sk first sc, sc in each of next 5 sc, ch 3, (sc in ch-7 sp, ch 3), continue in pat. Turn.

Row 38 Continue in pat, ending sk first sc, sc in each of next 3 sc, ch 2, sc in top of turning ch. Turn.

Row 39 Ch 3, sk 2 sc, sc in next sc, continue in pat. Turn.

Rows 40–56 Repeat rows 32–39 two more times. Then repeat row 32 one more time. Turn.

Ribbon Row

Row 57 Ch 4, (dc in ch-7 sp, ch 1) 2x, dc in next sc, *(ch 1, sk 1 sc, dc in next sc) 3x, (ch 1, dc in ch-7 sp) 3x. Repeat from * across, ending (ch1, dc in last 7 sp) 3x. Turn.

BODICE AND SHOULDER

Row 58 Ch 2, sc in first ch-1 sp, sc in next dc, sc in next ch-1 sp, *ch 3, sk 1 ch-1 sp, sc in next ch-1 sp, ch 3, sc in next ch-1 sp, ch 3, sk 1 ch-1 sp, sc in next ch-1 sp, (sc in next dc, sc in next ch-1 sp) 2x. Repeat from * across ending row with ch 3, sk 1 ch-1 sp, 3 sc in ch-4 sp. Turn.

Row 59 Ch 2, sc in each of next 2 sc, ch 3, sk (sc, ch-3, sc), sc in each of next 3 sc, ch 3, sk ch-3 sp, 7 dc in next ch-3 sp, continue in pat, ending ch 3, sc in each of last 2 sc. Turn.

Row 60 Ch 3, sc in each of next 7 dc, continue in pat, ending ch 3, sk 1 sc, sc in next sc. Turn.

Row 61 Ch 7, sk first sc, sc in each of next 7 sc, continue in pat, ending sc in each of next 7 sc, sc in turning ch. Turn.

Row 62 Ch 3, sk first 2 sc, sc in each of next 5 sc, continue in pat, ending ch 3, sc in turning ch. Turn

Row 63 Ch 5, sk first ch-3 sp, 7 dc in next ch-3 sp, continue in pat, ending sk first sc, sc in next 3 sc. Turn.

Row 64 Ch 3, sk first sc, sc in next sc, continue in pat, ending ch 3, sc in turning ch. Turn.

Row 65 Ch 3, sc in each of next 7 sc, continue in pat, ending ch 7, sc in turning ch. Turn.

Row 66 Ch 3, sc in ch-7 sp, sk 1 sc, sc in next 5 sc, continue in pat, ending ch 3, sc in ch-3 sp, ch 3, sc in turning ch. Turn.

Row 67 Ch 4, 3 dc in first ch-3 sp, ch 3, continue in pat, ending 4 dc in last ch-3 sp. Turn.

Row 68 Ch 2, sc in each of the next 4 dc, ch 3, continue in pat, ending ch 3, sc in turning ch. Turn.

Row 69 Ch 7, sk (ch-3 sp, sc, ch-3 sp), sc in each of the next 7 sc, continue in pat, ending sc in each of next 3 sc. Turn.

Row 70 Ch 2, sk 1 sc, sc in each of the next 2 sc, ch 3, sc in ch-7 sp, continue in pat, ending sc in first ch of turning ch. Turn.

Row 71 Ch 2, sk first ch-3 sp, 4 dc in next ch-3 sp, continue in pat, ending sk first ch-3 sp, 7 dc in next ch-3 sp, ch 3, sc in last sc. Turn.

Row 72 Ch 3, sk 1 dc, sc in each of next 6 dc, continue in pat, ending sk 1 dc, sc in each of next 2 dc. Turn.

Row 73 Ch 2, sc in first 2 sc, ch 7, continue in pat, ending sk first sc, sc in each of next 5 sc. Turn.

Row 74 Ch 2, sk first sc, sc in each of next 3 sc, ch 3, continue in pat, ending ch 3, (sc in ch-7 sp, ch 3) 2x, sc in last sc. Turn.

Row 75 Ch 4, sk first ch-3 sp, 7 dc in next ch-3 sp, ch 3, continue in pat, ending sk 1 sc, sc in each of next 2 sc, sc in turning ch. Turn.

Row 76 Ch 2, sk 1 sc, sc in next sc, ch 3, continue in pat, ending sc in each of next 7 dc. Turn.

Row 77 Ch 2, sc in each of next 7 sc, continue in pat, ending ch 3, sc in last sc. Turn.

Row 78 Ch 3, sc in ch-3 sp, ch 3, sk 1 sc, sc in each of next 5 sc, continue in pat, ending sk next sc, sc in each of next 5 sc. Turn.

Row 79 Ch 2, sk first sc, sc in next 3 sc, ch 3, continue in pat, ending 3 dc in last ch-3 sp. Turn.

Row 80 Ch 2, sk first dc, sc in each of next 2 dc, ch 7, continue in pat, ending ch 7, sc in turning ch. Turn.

Row 81 Ch 2, (sc in ch-7 sp, ch 3) 2x, continue in pat, ending ch 3, sk first sc, sc in next 2 sc. Turn.

Row 82 Ch 2, sc in first sc, ch 3, continue in pat, ending sk next ch-3 sp, 7 dc in next ch-3 sp. Turn.

Row 83 Ch 2, sk first dc, sc in each of next 6 dc, continue in pat, ending ch 3, sc in turning ch. Turn.

Row 84 Ch 4, sk first sc, sc in each of next 5 sc, continue in pat, ending sc in each of last 6 sc. Turn.

Row 85 Ch 2, sc in each of first 6 sc, continue in pat, ending ch 3, sc in turning ch. Turn.

Row 86 Ch 3, sc in first ch-3 sp, ch 3, sk 1 sc, sc in next 5 sc, continue in pat, ending sk 1 sc, sc in each of next 5 sc. Turn.

Row 87 Ch 2, sk 1 sc, sc in each of next 3 sc, ch 3, continue in pat, ending 3 dc in first ch-3 sp. Turn.

Row 88 Ch 2, sk 1 dc, sc in each of next 2 dc, ch 3, continue in pat, ending ch 3, sk first sc, sc in next sc, ch 3, sc in turning ch. Turn.

Row 89 Ch 7, sk (ch-3, sc, ch-3), sc in each of next 7 sc, continue in pat, ending ch 7, sc in each of next 2 sc, sc in turning ch. Turn.

Row 90 Ch 2, sk first sc, sc in next sc, ch 3, sc in ch-7 sp, continue in pat, ending ch 3 (sc, ch 3) 2x in last ch-7 sp. Turn.

Row 91 Ch 4, sk first ch-3 sp, 7 dc in next ch-3 sp, continue in pat, ending ch 3, sc in last sc, sc in turning ch. Turn.

Row 92 Ch 4, sc in each of next 7 dc, continue in pat, ending sc in each of next 7 dc. Turn.

LG/XL Only
Repeat rows 85–92 one more time.
Fasten off.

RIGHT FRONT
Note Right Front is worked on 4 (5) repeats. Ch 51 (63) + 2.

Rows 1–23 Work rows 1–15 in pat once, then work rows 8–15 in pattern once. Turn.

LG/XL Only
Work rows 8–15 in pat stitch once more.

Row 24 Ch 2, sc in each of the next 2 sc, ch 7, sk (ch-3, sc, ch-3), sc in each of the next 7 sc, continue in established pat. Turn.

Row 25 Continue in pat, ending ch 3, (sc in ch-7 sp, ch 3) 2x, sk 1 sc, sc in next 2 sc. Turn.

Row 26 Ch 4, sk next ch-3 sp, 7 dc in next ch-3 sp, continue in pat. Turn.

Row 27 Continue in pat, ending sc in each of the next 7 dc, ch 2, sc in turning ch. Turn.

Row 28 Ch 2, sc in each of the next 7 sc, continue in pat. Turn.

Row 29 Ch 3, sk first sc, sc in each of the next 5 sc, continue in pat. Turn.

Row 30 Ch 3, 3 dc in first ch-3 sp, continue in pat, ending ch 3, 2 dc in turning ch. Turn.

Row 31 Ch 2, sk first dc, sc in next dc, continue in pat, ending sc in each of last 3 dc, sc in turning ch. Turn.

Row 32 Ch 2, sk 1 sc, sc in each of next 2 sc, continue in pat, ending ch 7, sc in last sc, sc in turning ch. Turn.

Row 33 Ch 2, (sc in ch-7 sp, ch 3) 2x, continue in pat, ending ch 3, skip 1 sc, sc in each of next 2 sc, sc in turning ch. Turn.

Row 34 Ch 2, sc in each of next 2 sc, ch 3, continue in pat, ending ch 3, sc in last sc. Turn.

Row 35 Ch 4, sc in each of next 7 dc, continue in pat, ending ch 3, sc in turning ch. Turn.

Winter Lace Cardi

Row 36 Ch 4, sk 1 sc, sc in each of next 6 sc, continue in pat, ending ch 3, sc in turning ch. Turn.

Row 37 Ch 4, sc in ch-3 sp, ch 3, sk 1 sc, sc in each of next 5 sc, continue in pat, ending ch 3, sc in turning ch. Turn.

Row 38 Ch 4, sk 1 sc, sc in each of next 3 sc, continue in pat, ending 4 dc in last ch-3 sp. Turn.

Row 39 Ch 2, sc in each of next 4 dc, continue in pat, ending sk 1 sc, sc in next sc, ch 3, sc in turning ch. Turn.

Rows 40–56 Repeat rows 32–39 two more times, then repeat row 32 one more time. Turn.

Ribbon Row

Row 57 Ch 4, dc in ch-3 sp, ch 1, *(sk 1 sc, dc in next sc, ch 1) 4x, (dc in next ch-7 sp, ch 1) 3x, ch 1. Repeat from * across, ending (dc in next sc, ch 1, sk 1 sc) 2x, dc in turning ch. Turn.

BODICE AND SHOULDER

Row 58 Ch 3, sc in first dc, ch 3, sk one dc, sc in next ch-1 sp, *(sc in next dc, sc in next ch-1 sp) 2x, ch 3, sk 2 dc, sc in next ch-1 sp, ch 3, sc in next ch-1 sp, ch 3, sk 2 dc, sc in next ch-1 sp. Repeat from * across, ending sc in next dc, sc in turning ch. Turn.

Row 59 Ch 2, sc in next sc, ch 3, sk ch-3 sp, 7 dc in next ch-3 sp, continue in pat, ending ch 3, sk ch-3 sp, 3 dc in next ch-3 sp. Turn.

Row 60 Ch 2, sc in each of next 3 dc, ch 3, continue in pat, ending with sc in each of next 3 dc, ch 2, sc in turning ch. Turn.

Row 61 Ch 2, sc in each of the next 7 sc, continue in pat, ending sc in last 3 sc. Turn.

Row 62 Ch 2, sc in each of first 2 sc, ch 3, continue in pat, ending sk first sc, sc in each of next 5 sc. Turn.

Row 63 Ch 3, sk 1 sc, sc in each of next 3 sc, continue in pat, ending ch 3, sk first sc, sc in next sc. Turn.

Row 64 Ch 3, sc in each each of next 7 dc, continue in pat, ending ch 3, sk first sc, sc in next sc, ch 3, sc in turning ch. Turn.

Row 65 Ch 7, continue in pat, ending ch 7, sk one sc, sc in next sc. Turn.

Row 66 Ch 3, sc in ch-7 sp, continue in pat, ending (ch 3, sc in ch-7 sp) 2x. Turn.

Row 67 Ch 4, 3 dc in ch-3 sp, ch 3, continue in pat, ending ch 3, 3 dc in last ch-3 sp. Turn.

Row 68 Ch 2, sk 1 dc, sc in each of next 2 dc, continue in pat, ending sc in each of next 3 dc. Turn.

Row 69 Ch 2, sk first sc, sc in next sc, ch 7, continue in pat, ending ch 7, sc in turning ch. Turn.

Row 70 Ch 3, sc in ch-7 sp, ch 3, sk 1 sc, sc in next 5 sc, continue in pat, ending ch 3, sc in turning ch. Turn.

Row 71 Ch 3, sk first ch-3 sp, 7 dc in next ch-3 sp, continue in pat, ending ch 3, 4 dc in ch-3 sp. Turn.

Row 72 Ch 2, sk first dc, sc in each of next 3 dc, ch 3, continue in pat, ending sc in each of next 6 dc. Turn.

Row 73 Ch 2, sk first sc, sc in each of next 5 sc, ch 7, continue in pat, ending sc in each of next 3 sc. Turn.

Row 74 Ch 2, sk first sc, sc in next sc, (ch 3, sc in ch-7 sp) 2x, continue in pat, ending ch 3, sk 1 sc, sc in each of next 4 sc. Turn.

Row 75 Ch 2, sc in each of first 3 sc, ch 3, continue in pat, ending ch 3, sk first ch-3 sp, 7 dc in next ch-3 sp, ch 3, sc in turning ch. Turn.

Row 76 Ch 2, sc in each of next 7 dc, ch 3, continue in pat, ending ch 3, sk 1 sc, sc in next sc. Turn.

Row 77 Ch 3, sc in each of next 7 sc, continue in pat, ending sc in each of last 7 sc. Turn.

Row 78 Ch 2, sk first sc, sc in each of next 5 sc, ch 3, continue in pat, ending (ch 3, sc in ch-3 sp) 2x. Turn.

Row 79 Ch 4, 2 dc in first ch-3 sp, sk (sc, ch-3, sc), sk one more sc, sc in each of next 3 sc, continue in pat, ending ch 3, sk one sc, sc in each of next 4 sc. Turn.

Row 80 Ch 3, sk 2 sc, sc in next sc, ch 3, continue in pat, ending ch 3, sc in each of next 2 sc. Turn.

Row 81 Ch 2, sc in each of first 2 sc, ch 7, continue in pat, ending ch 7, sc in turning ch. Turn.

Row 82 Ch 2, (sc in ch-7 sp, ch 3) 2x, continue in pat, ending ch 3, sk 1 sc, sc in next sc, sc in turning ch. Turn.

Row 83 Ch 3, sk first ch-3 sp, 7 dc in next ch-3 sp, continue in pat, ending sk one ch-3 sp, 7 dc in next ch-3 sp. Turn.

Row 84 Ch 2, sc in each of first 7 dc, continue in pat, ending 7 sc in each of next 7 dc, ch 1, sc in turning ch. Turn.

Row 85 Ch 3, sc in each of next 7 sc, continue in pat, ending 7 sc in each of last 7 dc. Turn.

Row 86 Ch 2, sc in each of first 6 sc, continue in pat, ending (ch 3, sc in ch-3 sp) 2x. Turn.

Row 87 Ch 4, 3 dc in first ch-3 sp, continue in pat, ending ch 3, sc in turning ch. Turn.

Row 88 Ch 3, sk 1 sc, sc in next sc, ch 3, continue in pat, ending ch 3, sc in each of next 3 dc. Turn.

Row 89 Ch 2, sk 1 sc, sc in each of next 2 sc, ch 7, continue in pat, ending ch 7, sc in turning ch. Turn.

Row 90 (Ch 3, sc in ch-7 sp) 2x, ch 3, continue in pat, ending ch 3, sk 1 sc, sc in next sc, sc in turning ch. Turn.

Row 91 Ch 2, sk first ch-3 sp, 7 dc in next ch-3 sp, continue in pat, ending sk first ch-3 sp, 7 dc in next ch-3 sp, ch 2, sc in turning ch. Turn.

Row 92 Ch 2, sc in each of next 7 dc, continue in pat, ending sc in last 7 dc.

LG/XL Only

Repeat rows 85–92 one more time. Fasten off.

SLEEVES (MAKE TWO)

Ch 51 (63) + 2.

Rows 1–15 Work in pat. Turn

Row 16–47 Repeat rows 8–15 4 times. Turn.

LG/XL Only

Repeat rows 8–15 one more time. Turn.

Rows 48–52 Repeat rows 8–12 one time. Turn.

Row 53 Ch 2, sk first sc, sc in next 5 sc, ch 3, continue in pat, ending ch 3, sk next sc, sc in next 5 sc. Turn.

Row 54 Ch 2, sk first sc, sc in each of next 3 sc, continue in pat, ending sk next sc, sc in each of next 3 sc. Turn.

Row 55 Sk first sc, sc in next sc, continue in pat, ending sk first sc, sc in next sc. Turn.
Row 56 Ch 4, sc in each of next 7 sc, continue in pat, ending sc in each of next 7 sc, ch 3, sc in next sc. Turn.
Row 57 Ch 3, sc in next ch 3 sp, ch 3, sk one sc, sc in each of the next 5 sc, continue in pat, ending ch 3, sc in top of turning ch. Turn.
Row 58 Ch 4, 3 dc in first ch-3 sp, ch 3, sk one sc, sc in each of next 3 sc, continue in pat, ending 4 dc in last ch-3 sp. Turn.
Row 59 Ch 2, sc in each of next 3 dc, ch 3, sk next sc, sc in next sc, continue in pat, ending ch 3, sc in each of next 3 dc. Turn.
Row 60 Ch 2, sc in each of next 2 sc, ch 7, continue in pat, ending ch 7, sc in each of next 2 sc. Turn.
Row 61 Ch 2, sc in first sc, ch 3, sc in ch-7 sp, continue in pat, ending ch 3, sk next sc, sc in next sc. Turn.
Row 62 Ch 3, sk first ch-3 sp, 7dc in next ch-3 sp, continue in pat, ending sk ch-3, ch 2, sc in next sc. Turn.
Row 63 Ch 2, sk first sc, sc in each of the next 6 dc, continue in pat, ending sc in each of the next 6 dc. Turn.
Row 64 Ch 2, sk first sc, sc in each of the next 4 sc, continue in pat, ending sk first sc, sc in each of the next 4 sc. Turn.
Row 65 Ch 2, sk first sc, sc in each of the next 3 sc, continue in pat, ending sk first sc, sc in each of the next 3 sc. Turn.

Row 66 Ch 2, sk first sc, sc in next sc, continue in pat, ending sk first sc, sc in next sc. Turn.
Row 67 Ch 2, sc in first sc, ch 3, continue in pat, ending ch 3, sc in next sc. Fasten off.

Bottom Sleeve Ruffle
With wrong side of sleeve facing, connect yarn at right corner. Ch 2.
Row 1 Follow pat row 1. Turn.
Row 2 Follow pat row 2, working ch-5s instead of ch-3s. Turn.
Row 3 Follow pat row 3.
Row 4 Follow pat row 7, working ch-4s instead of ch-3s. Turn.
Row 5 Follow pat row 7, working ch-4s instead of ch-3s. Turn.
Row 6 Follow pat row 5. Turn.
Row 7 Follow pat row 2, working 10 dcs instead of 7 dcs. Turn.
Row 8 Follow pat row 3, working 10 scs in the dcs, and ch-6s in between.
Fasten off.

FINISHING

With right sides together, sew shoulder seams. Sew sleeves on, then sew the side seams of body and underarm seams of sleeves.

Edging
On the right side, join yarn at any corner. Work (sc, ch 3) evenly spaced around the bottom, front and back, so that the edging lies flat. Fasten off. Weave in all ends.

Ribbon
Fold ribbon in half lengthwise, to make it easier to weave through the stitches on the Ribbon row. Leaving approx 20"/51cm at the end, weave the ribbon under the side edge, (over 3 dcs, and under 1 dc), repeating to the opposite edge. If you wish, you may baste the ribbon at the side edges to hold in place. ▪

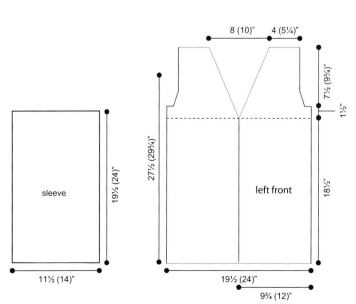

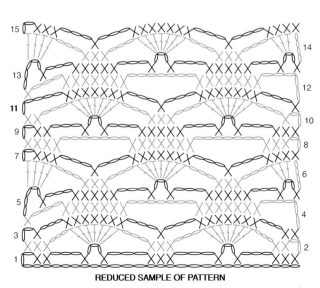

REDUCED SAMPLE OF PATTERN

Kimono Cardi

STITCH GLOSSARY

CI (cluster) Yo, insert hook in indicated st, yo and draw up a loop, [yo, insert hook in same st, yo and draw up a loop] twice, yo and draw through all 7 loops on hook, ch 1.

SIZES

S (M, L, 1X, 2X)

FINISHED MEASUREMENTS

Chest 36 (42, 44, 49, 51)"/91.5 (106.5, 111.5, 124.5, 129.5)cm
Length 25 (27, 27, 29, 30)"/63.5 (68.5, 68.5, 73.5, 76)cm

GAUGE

3 pattern repeats (fans) = 5½"/14cm and 8 rows = 4"/10cm over soft fan pattern using size F/5 (3.75mm) crochet hook.
Remember to check gauge for best results!

PATTERN STITCH

Soft Fan Pattern (multiple of 10 sts + 1)
Row 1 (wrong side) Sc in 2nd ch from hook, *ch 3, sk 5 ch, dc in next ch, ch 5; working behind dc just made, dc in 4th ch of ch-5 just skipped; ch 3, sk 3 ch, sc in next ch; repeat from * across.

Row 2 (right side) Ch 3 (counts as first dc), turn, sk first ch-3 sp, 11 dc in next ch-5 sp (fan made), sk next ch-3 sp, *CI in next sc, ch 1, sk next ch-3 sp, 11 dc in next ch-5 sp (fan made), sk next ch-3 sp; repeat from * across, dc in last sc.
Row 3 Ch 2, turn, sk first 2 dc, hdc in next dc, ch 4, hdc in top of hdc just made, ch 3, sk 3 dc, sc in next dc, ch 3, *dc in 2nd dc of next 11-dc group, ch 5; working behind dc just made, dc in 10th dc of previous 11-dc group; ch 3, sk 3 dc, sc in next dc, ch 3; repeat from * across, dc in top of ch-3 turning ch, ch 2; working behind dc just made, work dc in 10th dc of previous 11-dc group.
Row 4 Ch 3 (counts as first dc), turn, sk first st, 5 dc in next ch-2 sp, sk next ch-3 sp, CI in next sc, ch 1, sk next ch-3 sp, *11 dc in next ch-5 sp (fan made), sk next ch-3 sp, CI in next sc, ch 1, sk next ch-3 sp; repeat from * across, 5 dc in ch-4 sp, dc in top of ch-2 turning ch.
Row 5 Ch 1, turn, sc in first st, ch 3, dc in 2nd dc of next 11-dc group, ch 5; working behind dc just made, dc in 5th dc of previous 6-dc group, ch 3, *sk 3 dc, sc in next dc, ch 3, dc in 2nd dc of next dc group, ch 5; working behind dc just made, dc in 10th dc of previous dc group, ch 3; repeat from * across, sk last 3 dc, sc in top of ch-3 turning ch.
Repeat Rows 2–5 for pattern.

NOTE

Cuffs are first worked from wrist toward the hands. The Sleeves are then worked beginning at the wrist and working toward the shoulder. Similarly, the hem is first worked toward the lower edge. The Back and Fronts are then worked beginning at the top edge of the hem and working toward the shoulders and neck.

SLEEVE (MAKE 2)

Beginning at wrist of cuff, ch 102 (112, 112, 122, 132).
Rows 1–5 Work Rows 1–5 of soft fan pattern—10 (11, 11, 12, 13) fans.
Rows 6–8 Work Rows 2–4 of soft fan pattern.
Fasten off.

Begin Sleeve At Wrist

From right side, join yarn in first ch of cuff foundation ch.
Row 1 Ch 3 (counts as first dc), turn, sk first ch-sp, 11 dc in sp beneath next fan formed by crossed dc, sk next ch-sp, *CI in ch beneath next CI, ch 1, sk next ch-sp, 11 dc in sp beneath next fan formed by crossed dc, sk next ch-sp; repeat from * across, dc in last ch—10 (11, 11, 12, 13) fans.
Row 2 Work Row 3 of soft fan pattern. Continue in soft fan pattern until sleeve measures 12 (13, 13, 14, 14)"/30.5 (33, 33, 35.5, 35.5)cm from beginning. End with Row 2 of pattern.

Shape Sleeve Cap

Row 1 Ch 7, turn, sc in 6th dc of next 11-dc group, *ch 3, dc in 2nd dc of next 11-dc group, ch 5; working behind dc just made, dc in 10th dc of previous 11-dc group; ch 3, sk 3 dc, sc in next dc; repeat from * across.
Row 2 Ch 3, turn, sk first ch-3 sp, 5 dc in first ch-5 sp, sk next ch-3 sp, CI in next sc, ch 1, sk next ch-3 sp, *11 dc in next ch-5 sp, sk next ch-3 sp, CI in next sc, ch 1, sk next ch-3 sp; repeat from * across to last ch-5 sp, 6 dc in last ch-5 sp, ch 3, sk next ch-3 sp, sc in last sc; leave last ch-7 sp unworked—8 (9, 9, 10, 11) fans.
Finishing Row Ch 7, turn, sk 2 dc, sc in next dc, ch 2, dc in CI, ch 2, sk 2 dc, hdc in next dc, *ch 2, sk 2 dc, sc in next dc, ch 2, sk 2 dc, hdc in next dc, ch 2, dc in CI, ch 2, sk 2 dc, hdc in next dc; repeat from * to last dc group, ch 7, sc in base of ch-3 turning ch. Fasten off.

BACK

Beginning at top of hem, ch 102 (112, 122, 132, 142).
Rows 1–5 Work Rows 1–5 of soft fan pattern—10 (11, 12, 13, 14) fans.
Rows 6–8 Work Rows 2–4 of soft fan pattern.
Fasten off.

Begin Back At Top Edge Of Hem

From right side, join yarn in first ch of hem foundation ch.
Row 1 Ch 3 (counts as first dc), turn, sk first

ch-sp, 11 dc in sp beneath next fan formed by crossed dc, sk next ch-sp, *Cl in ch beneath next Cl, ch 1, sk next ch-sp, 11 dc in sp beneath next fan formed by crossed dc, sk next ch-sp; repeat from * across, dc in last ch—10 (11, 12, 13, 14) fans.

Row 2 Work Row 3 of soft fan pattern. Continue in soft fan pattern until Back measures 16 (17, 17, 18, 18)"/40.5 (43, 43, 45.5, 45.5) cm from beginning. End with Row 2 of pattern.

Shape Armhole

Row 1 Ch 7, turn, sc in 6th dc of next 11-dc group, *ch 3, dc in 2nd dc of next 11-dc group, ch 5; working behind dc just made, dc in 10th dc of previous 11-dc group; ch 3, sk 3 dc, sc in next dc; repeat from * across.

Row 2 Ch 3, turn, sk first ch-3 sp, 5 dc in first ch-5 sp, sk next ch-3 sp, Cl in next sc, ch 1, sk next ch-3 sp, *11 dc in next ch-5 sp, sk next ch-3 sp, Cl in next sc, ch 1, sk next ch-3 sp; repeat from * across to last ch-5 sp, 6 dc in last ch-5 sp, ch 3, sk next ch-3 sp, sc in last sc—8 (9, 10, 11, 12) fans.

Row 3 Ch 7, turn, dc in 2nd dc of next 11-dc group, ch 5; working behind dc just made, dc in 5th dc of previous 6-dc group, *ch 3, sk 3 dc, sc in next dc, ch 3, dc in 2nd dc of next dc group, ch 5; working behind dc just made, dc in 10th dc of previous dc group; repeat from * across to last dc group, ch 3, sk 2 dc, sl st in last dc.

Row 4 Ch 3, 5 dc in first ch-5 sp, sk next ch-3 sp, Cl in next sc, ch 1, sk next ch-3 sp, *11 dc in next ch-5 sp, sk next ch-3 sp, Cl in next sc, ch 1, sk next ch-3 sp; repeat from * across to last ch-5 sp, 6 dc in last ch-5 sp.

Row 5 Work Row 5 of soft fan pattern. Continue in soft fan pattern until armhole measures 9 (10, 10, 11, 12)"/23 (25.5, 25.5, 28, 30.5)cm. End with Row 4 of pattern.

Finishing Row Ch 7, turn, sk 2 dc, sc in next dc, ch 2, dc in Cl, ch 2, sk 2 dc, hdc in next dc, *ch 2, sk 2 dc, sc in next dc, ch 2, sk 2 dc, hdc in next dc, ch 2, dc in Cl, ch 2, sk 2 dc, hdc in next dc; repeat from * to last dc group, ch 7, sc in base of ch-3 turning ch.
Fasten off.

LEFT FRONT

Beginning at top of hem, ch 52 (62, 62, 72, 72).

Rows 1–5 Work Rows 1–5 of soft fan pattern—5 (6, 6, 7, 7) fans.

Rows 6–8 Work Rows 2–4 of soft fan pattern.
Fasten off.

Begin Left Front At Top Edge Of Hem

From right side, join yarn in first ch of hem foundation ch.

Row 1 Ch 3 (counts as first dc), turn, sk first ch-sp, 11 dc in sp beneath next fan formed by crossed dc, sk next ch-sp, *Cl in ch beneath next Cl, ch 1, sk next ch-sp, 11 dc in sp beneath next fan formed by crossed dc, sk next ch-sp; repeat from * across, dc in last ch—5 (6, 6, 7, 7) fans.

Row 2 Work Row 3 of soft fan pattern. Continue in soft fan pattern until left front measures 14 (15, 15, 16, 16)"/ 35.5 (38, 38, 40.5, 40.5)cm from beginning. End with Row 2 of pattern.

Shape Neck and Armhole

Row 1 (wrong side) Ch 7, turn, sc in 6th dc of next 11-dc group, *ch 3, dc in 2nd dc of next 11-dc group, ch 5; working behind dc just made, dc in 10th dc of previous 11-dc group; ch 3, sk 3 dc, sc in next dc, ch 3; repeat from * across, dc in top of ch-3 turning ch, ch 2; working behind dc just made, work dc in 10th dc of previous 11-dc group.

Row 2 Ch 3 (counts as first dc), turn, sk first st, 5 dc in next ch-2 sp, sk next ch-3 sp, Cl in next sc, ch 1, sk next ch-3 sp, *11 dc in next ch-5 sp, sk next ch-3 sp, Cl in next sc, ch 1, sk next ch-3 sp; repeat from * across to last ch-5 sp, 6 dc in last ch-5 sp, sc in last sc; leave last ch-7 sp unworked.

Row 3 (wrong side) Ch 7, dc in 2nd dc of next 11-dc group, ch 5; working behind dc just made, dc in 5th dc of previous 6-dc group, ch 3, *sk 3 dc, sc in next dc, ch 3, dc in 2nd dc of next dc group, ch 5; working behind dc just made, dc in 10th dc of previous dc group, ch 3; repeat from * across, sk last 3 dc, sc in top of ch-3 turning ch.

Row 4 Ch 3, 5 dc in first ch-5 sp, sk next ch-3 sp, Cl in next sc, ch 1, sk next ch-3 sp, *11 dc in next ch-5 sp, sk next ch-3 sp, Cl in next sc, ch 1, sk next ch-3 sp; repeat from * across to last ch-5 sp, 11 dc in last ch-5 sp, dc in 4th ch of ch-7 turning ch.

Row 5 Ch 2, turn, sk first 2 dc, hdc in next dc, ch 4, hdc in top of hdc just made, ch 3, *sk 3 dc, sc in next dc, ch 3, dc in 2nd dc of next dc group, ch 5; working behind dc just made, dc in 10th dc of previous dc group, ch 3; repeat from * across, sk last 3 dc, sc in top of ch-3 turning ch.

Row 6 Ch 3 (counts as first dc), turn, sk first ch-3 sp, 11 dc in next ch-5 sp, sk next ch-3 sp, Cl in next sc, ch 1, sk next ch-3 sp, *11 dc in next ch-5 sp, sk next ch-3 sp, Cl in next sc, ch 1, sk next ch-3 sp; repeat from * across, 5 dc in ch-4 sp, dc in top of ch-2 turning ch—3 (4, 4, 5, 5) fans.

Row 7 Ch 1, turn, sc in first st, ch 3, dc in 2nd dc of next 11-dc group, ch 5; working behind dc just made, dc in 5th dc of previous 6-dc group, ch 3, sk 3 dc, sc in next dc, ch 3, *dc in 2nd dc of next dc group, ch 5; working behind dc just made, dc in 10th dc of previous dc group, ch 3, sk 3 dc, sc in next dc, ch 3; repeat from * across, dc in top of ch-3 turning ch, ch 2; working behind dc just made, work dc in 10th dc of previous 11-dc group.

Row 8 Ch 3 (counts as first dc), turn, sk first st, 5 dc in next ch-2 sp, sk next ch-3 sp, Cl in next sc, ch 1, sk next ch-3 sp, 11 dc in next ch-5 sp, sk next ch-3 sp, *Cl in next sc, ch 1, sk next ch-3 sp, 11 dc in

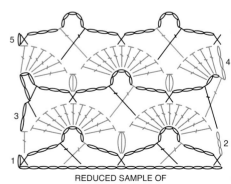

REDUCED SAMPLE OF SOFT FAN PATTERN

next ch-5 sp, sk next ch-3 sp; repeat from * across, dc in last sc.

Repeat Rows 5–8 until armhole measures same as Back armhole.

Finishing Row Ch 7, turn, sk 5 dc, sc in next dc, sk 2 dc, hdc in next dc, ch 2, dc in Cl, ch 2, sk 2 dc, hdc in next dc, *ch 2, sk 2 dc, sc in next dc, ch 2, sk 2 dc, hdc in next dc, ch 2, dc in Cl, ch 2, sk 2 dc, hdc in next dc; repeat from * to last dc group, ch 7, sc in base of ch-3 turning ch.
Fasten off.

RIGHT FRONT

Work as for Left Front, reversing shaping.

BELT

Ch 8.

Row 1 Sc in 2nd ch from hook and each ch across—7 sc.

Rows 2 and 3 Ch 1, turn, sc in each sc across.

Row 4 Ch 2, hdc in first sc, [ch 1, sk 1 sc, hdc in next sc] 3 times.

Row 5 Ch 1, turn, sc in each hdc and ch-1 sp across.

Repeat Rows 3–5 until belt measures 48"/122cm.

FINISHING

Block lightly to measurements. Sew shoulder seams. Sew sleeves into armholes. Sew side and sleeve seams.

Front and Neck Edging

With right side facing, join yarn in right front and lower edge.

Row 1 Ch 1, sc in same sp, work 241 sc evenly spaced around right front, neck, and left front edge.

Row 2 Ch 1, turn, sc in first sc, *ch 3, sk 5 sc, dc in next sc, ch 5; working behind dc just made, dc in 4th sc of 5 sc just skipped; ch 3, sk 3 sc, sc in next sc; repeat from * across.

Row 3 Work Row 2 of soft fan pattern.
Fasten off.

Weave in all ends. ▪

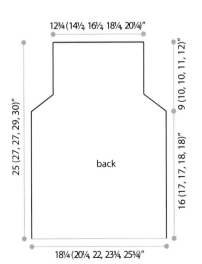

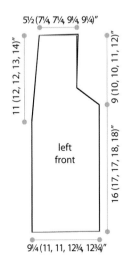

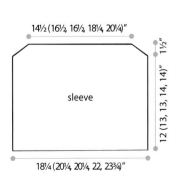

12¾ (14½, 16½, 18¼, 20¼)"

9 (10, 10, 11, 12)"

25 (27, 27, 29, 30)"

16 (17, 17, 18, 18)"

back

18¼ (20¼, 22, 23¾, 25¾)"

5½ (7¼, 7¼, 9¼, 9¼)"

11 (12, 12, 13, 14)"

9 (10, 10, 11, 12)"

16 (17, 17, 18, 18)"

left front

9¼ (11, 11, 12¾, 12¾)"

14½ (16½, 16½, 18¼, 20¼)"

1½"

12 (13, 13, 14, 14)"

sleeve

18¼ (20¼, 20¼, 22, 23¾)"

Ruffles Jacket

MATERIALS

Yarn (4)

RED HEART® *Soft Yarn*, 5oz/140g skeins, each approx 256yd/234m (acrylic)

- 4 (5, 6) skeins #4601 Off White

Hook

- Size H/8 (5mm) crochet hook *or size to obtain gauge*

Notions

- 7½ (9, 10½) yards/7 (8½, 9½) meters of 1½" velvet ribbon in Burgundy
- 3½ (4, 5) yards/3¼ (3½, 4½) meters ⅝" double-faced satin ribbon in Burgundy
- Sewing thread in off-white
- Sewing needle

SIZES
S (M, L)

FINISHED MEASUREMENTS
Bust 36 (40, 44)"/91.5 (101.5, 112)cm
Length 19 (20, 21)"/48 (51, 56)cm

NOTE
Measurements as shown in schematics do not include edging. Edging adds 1½" to sleeve and body lengths.

GAUGE
13 sts and 7 rows = 4" (10cm) over pattern st using size H/8 (5mm) crochet hook. *Remember to check gauge for best results!*

BACK
Ch 58 (66, 74) and sc in 2nd ch from hook and in each ch across, 57 (65, 73) sc, turn. Begin pattern st and work until piece measures 10 (10½, 11)"/ 25.5 (26.5, 28)cm. Fasten off.

ARMHOLE
Join yarn to the first dc after shell (5th st), work across in pattern st until 4 sts rem. Continue in pattern st on 49 (58, 57) sts until armhole measures 7½ (8, 8½)"/19 (20.5, 21.5)cm. Fasten off.

LEFT FRONT
Ch 30 (34, 38) and sc in 2nd st and in each ch across—29 (33, 37) sc. Turn. Begin pattern st and work until piece measures 10 (10½, 11)"/25.5 (26.5, 28)cm.

ARMHOLE
Work across to last 4 (4, 8) sts, turn. Continue in pattern st on 25 (29, 29) sts until armhole measures 2"/5cm, ending at armhole edge.

Neck Shaping
Work across to last 4 sts, turn. Continue in pattern st on 21 (25, 25) sts, dec 1 st at neck edge every row until 13 (14, 14) sts rem. Work even until piece measures same as the back.

RIGHT FRONT
Work same as for left front, reversing all shaping.

SLEEVES
Ch 30 and sc in 2nd st and in each ch across, 29 sc. Begin pattern st and inc 1 st on each side every other row until you have 49 (53, 57) sts. Work even until piece measures 17 (17½, 19½)"/43 (44.5, 49.5)cm or to desired length. Fasten off.

FINISHING
Sew shoulder seams. Set sleeves into armholes. Sew sleeves and side seams.

EDGING
Join yarn at the bottom left front corner.
Rnd 1 Ch 2, hdc evenly around, working 3 hdc in each lower edge corner. Join with sl st to begin ch-2.
Rnd 2 Ch 2, *skip 2 sts, 5 dc in next st, skip 2 sts, 1 hdc in next st; repeat from * around. Work around each sleeve in the same manner, disregarding corner instructions.

RIBBON
Measure enough satin ribbon to go around each sleeve cuff plus an extra 2"/5cm. Weave the ribbon under and over Rnd 1 of edging around each sleeve. Measure enough satin ribbon to go around edge of cardigan body plus an extra 12"/30cm. Weave through Rnd 1 of edging.
Using a sewing machine or by hand, baste near edge of velvet ribbon and slightly gather. Measure enough to go around each sleeve plus an extra 1"/2.5cm. Sew onto each sleeve by hand, being careful not to pull too tightly. Measure enough velvet ribbon to go around edge of cardigan body plus an extra 1"/2.5cm. Sew onto edge of body. ■

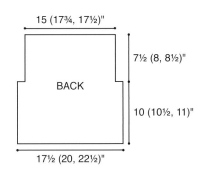

15 (17¾, 17½)"

7½ (8, 8½)"

BACK

10 (10½, 11)"

17½ (20, 22½)"

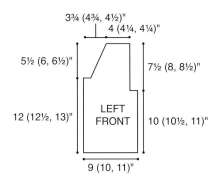

3¾ (4¾, 4½)"

4 (4¼, 4¼)"

5½ (6, 6½)"

7½ (8, 8½)"

LEFT FRONT

12 (12½, 13)"

10 (10½, 11)"

9 (10, 11)"

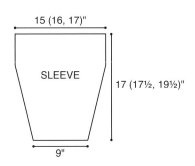

15 (16, 17)"

SLEEVE

17 (17½, 19½)"

9"

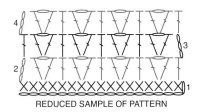

REDUCED SAMPLE OF PATTERN

19

Springtime Trench

MATERIALS

Yarn 4

RED HEART® *Super Saver® Economy*, 7oz/198g skeins, each approx 364yds/333m (acrylic)
• 6 (6, 6, 6) skeins #385 Royal

Hook
• Size I/9 (5.5mm) crochet hook *or size to obtain gauge*

Notions
• Yarn needle

STITCH GLOSSARY

hdc2tog (half double crochet 2 sts together) [Yo, insert hook in next st, yo and draw up a lp] twice; yo and draw through all 5 lps on hook.

SIZES
S (M, L, XL)

FINISHED MEASUREMENTS
Bust (wrapped and tied) 37 (40, 43, 45½)"/94 (101.5, 109, 114)cm
Length 32 (32½, 33, 33½)"/81.5 (82.5, 84, 85)cm

GAUGE
12 sts and 12 rows = 4"/10cm over pattern stitch using size I/9 (5.5mm) croochet hook. *Remember to check gauge for best results!*

NOTE
Each sc, hdc, dc, hdc2tog, and turning ch-2 counts as a st throughout.

BACK
Starting at bottom, ch 57 (61, 65, 69).
Row 1 (right side) Sc in 3rd ch from hook (2 skipped chs count as hdc); *dc in next ch, sc in next ch; repeat from * across to last 2 chs; dc in next ch, hdc in last ch—56 (60, 64, 68) sts. Ch 2 (counts as hdc on next row now and throughout), turn.

Row 2 Sk first hdc; *sc in next dc, dc in next sc; repeat from * across to skipped chs; hdc in first skipped ch. Ch 2, turn.
Row 3 Sk first hdc; *sc in next dc, dc in next sc; repeat from * across to turning ch; hdc in 2nd ch of turning ch-2. Ch 2, turn.
Repeat Row 3 until piece measures approx 13"/33cm from beginning, ending by working a wrong side row.

Waistline Shaping
Row 1 (right side) Sk first hdc, hdc2tog; sc in each dc and dc in each sc across to last 3 sts (including turning ch); hdc2tog, hdc in 2nd ch of turning ch-2—54 (58, 62, 66) sts. Ch 2, turn.
Rows 2–4 Sk first hdc, dc in next st; *sc in next dc, dc in next sc; repeat from * across to last 2 sts (including turning ch); sc in next st, hdc in 2nd ch of turning ch-2. Ch 2, turn.
Row 5 Repeat Row 1—52 (56, 60, 64) sts.
Rows 6–8 Sk first hdc, sc in next st; *dc in next sc, dc in next dc; repeat from * across to last 2 sts (including turning ch); dc in next st, hdc in 2nd ch of turning ch-2. Ch 2, turn.
Rows 9–12 Repeat Rows 1–4 once—50 (54, 58, 62) sts.
Row 13 Sk first hdc; *dc in next sc, sc in next dc; repeat from * across to turning ch; hdc in 2nd ch of turning ch-2. Ch 2, turn.
Repeat Row 13 until piece measures approx 19½ (20, 20, 20)"/49.5 (51, 51, 51) cm from beginning, ending by working a wrong side row.

Upper Body Shaping
Row 1 (right side) Hdc in first hdc; dc in each sc and sc in each dc across to turning ch; 2 hdc in 2nd ch of turning ch-2—52 (56, 60, 64) sts. Ch 2, turn.
Rows 2–4 Sk first hdc, sc in next st; *dc in next sc, sc in next dc; repeat from * across to last 2 sts (including turning ch); dc in next st, hdc in 2nd ch of turning ch-2. Ch 2, turn.
Row 5 Repeat Row 1—54 (58, 62, 66) sts.
Rows 6–8 Sk first hdc, dc in next st; *sc in next dc, dc in next sc; repeat from *

across to last 2 sts (including turning ch); sc in next st, hdc in 2nd ch of turning ch-2. Ch 2, turn.
Row 9 Repeat Row 1—56 (60, 64, 68) sts.
Repeat Row 2 until piece measures approx 24 (24, 24½, 24½)"/ 61 (61, 62, 62 cm from beginning, ending by working a wrong side row. At end of last row, do not ch 2. Turn.

Armhole Shaping
Row 1 (right side) Sl st in first 4 (5, 5, 6) sts, ch 2 (counts as first hdc); dc in each sc and sc in each dc across to last 3 (4, 4, 5) sts—50 (52, 56, 58) sts. Turn, leaving rem sts unworked.
Row 2 Sl st in first 3 sts, ch 2; dc in each sc and sc in each dc across to last 2 sts (including beginning ch-2)—46 (48, 52, 54) sts. Ch 2, turn, leaving rem sts unworked.
Rows 3 and 4 Sk first st, hdc2tog; dc in each sc and sc in each dc across to last 3 sts (including turning ch or beginning ch-2); hdc2tog, hdc in 2nd ch of turning ch-2 or beginning ch-2. At end of Row 4—42 (44, 48, 50) sts. Ch 2, turn.
Rows 5–6 (7, 8, 8) Repeat Row 3 two (3, 4, 4) times more. At end of last row—38 (38, 40, 42) sts.

For Sizes S, M and XL Only
Row 7 (8, 8) Sk first hdc, dc in next st; *sc in next dc, dc in next sc; repeat from * across to last 2 sts (including turning ch); sc in next st, hdc in 2nd ch of turning ch-2. Ch 2, turn.
Repeat Row 7 (8, 9) until piece measures approx 32 (32½, 33½)"/81.5 (82.5, 85)cm from beginning. At end of last row, do not ch 2. Fasten off.

For Size L Only
Row 9 Sk first hdc, sc in next st; *dc in next sc, sc in next dc; repeat from * across to last 2 sts (including turning ch); dc in next st, hdc in 2nd ch of turning ch-2. Ch 2, turn.
Repeat Row 9 until piece measures approx 33"/84cm from beginning. At end of last row, do not ch 2. Fasten off.

LEFT FRONT

Starting at bottom, ch 41 (43, 45, 47).
Row 1 (right side) Sc in 3rd ch from hook (2 skipped chs count as hdc); *dc in next ch, sc in next ch; repeat from * across to last 2 chs; dc in next ch, hdc in last ch—40 (42, 44, 46) sts. Ch 2 (counts as hdc on next row now and throughout), turn.
Row 2 Sk first hdc; *sc in next dc, dc in next sc; repeat from * across to skipped chs; hdc in first skipped ch. Ch 2, turn.
Row 3 Sk first hdc; *sc in next dc, dc in next sc; repeat from * across to turning ch; hdc in 2nd ch of turning ch-2. Ch 2, turn.
Repeat Row 3 until piece measures approx 13"/33cm from beginning, ending by working a wrong side row.

Waistline Shaping

Row 1 (right side) Sk first hdc; hdc2tog; sc in each dc and dc in each sc across to turning ch; hdc in 2nd ch of turning ch-2—39 (41, 43, 45) sts. Ch 2, turn.
Row 2 Sk first hdc; *sc in next dc, dc in next sc; repeat from * across to last 2 sts (including turning ch); sc in next st, hdc in 2nd ch of turning ch-2. Ch 2, turn.
Rows 3 and 4 Sk first hdc; dc in each sc and sc in each dc across to turning ch; hdc in 2nd ch of turning ch-2. Ch 2, turn.
Row 5 Repeat Row 1—38 (40, 42, 44) sts.
Row 6 Sk first hdc; *sc in next dc, dc in next sc; repeat from * across to last 3 sts (including turning ch); sc in next dc, dc in next sc, hdc in 2nd ch of turning ch-2. Ch 2, turn.
Rows 7 and 8 Repeat Row 3 two times more.
Rows 9 and 10 Repeat Rows 1 and 2—37 (39, 41, 43) sts.
Repeat Row 3 until piece measures approx 19½ (20, 20, 20)"/49.5 (51, 51, 51)cm from beginning, ending by working a wrong side row.

Upper Body Shaping

Row 1 (right side) Hdc in first hdc; dc in each sc and sc in each dc across to turning ch; hdc in 2nd ch of turning ch-2—38 (40, 42, 44) sts. Ch 2, turn.

Row 2 Sk first hdc; *sc in next dc, dc in next sc; repeat from * across to last 3 sts (including turning ch); sc in next dc, dc in next st, hdc in 2nd ch of turning ch-2. Ch 2, turn.
Rows 3 and 4 Sk first hdc; sc in each dc and dc in each sc across to turning ch; hdc in 2nd ch of turning ch-2. Ch 2, turn.
Row 5 Repeat Row 1—39 (41, 43, 45) sts.
Row 6 Sk first hdc; *sc in next dc, dc in next sc; repeat from * across to last 2 sts (including turning ch); sc in next st, hdc in 2nd ch of turning ch-2. Ch 2, turn.
Rows 7 and 8 Repeat Row 3 two times more.
Rows 9 and 10 Repeat Rows 1 and 2—40 (42, 44, 46) sts.
Repeat row 3 until piece measures approx 24 (24, 24½, 24½)"/61 (61, 62, 62)cm from beginning, ending by working a wrong side row. At end of last row, do not ch 2. Turn.

Armhole Shaping

Row 1 (right side) Sl st in first 4 (5, 5, 6) sts, ch 2 (counts as first hdc); dc in each sc and sc in each dc across to turning ch; hdc in 2nd ch of turning ch-2—37 (38, 40, 41) sts. Ch 2, turn.
Row 2 Sk first hdc; sc in each dc and dc in each sc across to last 2 sts (including beginning ch-2)—35 (36, 38, 39) sts. Ch 2, turn, leaving rem sts unworked.
Row 3 Sk first st, hdc2tog; dc in each sc and sc in each dc across to turning ch; hdc in 2nd ch of turning ch-2—34 (35, 37, 38) sts. Ch 2, turn.
Row 4 Sk first hdc; sc in each dc and dc in each sc across to last 3 sts (including turning ch); hdc2tog, hdc in 2nd ch of turning ch-2—33 (34, 36, 37) sts. Ch 2, turn.

For Size S Only

Rows 5 and 6 Repeat Rows 3 and 4. At end of Row 6—31 sts.
Row 7 Sk first hdc, dc in next st; sc in each dc and dc in each sc across to turning ch; hdc in 2nd ch of turning ch-2. Ch 2, turn.

For Size M Only

Rows 5–7 Repeat Rows 3 and 4 once, then repeat Row 3 once more. At end of Row 7—31 sts.
Row 8 Sk first hdc; *sc in next dc, dc in next sc; repeat from * across to last 2 sts (including turning ch); sc in next st, hdc in 2nd ch of turning ch-2. Ch 2, turn.

For Size L Only

Rows 5–8 Repeat Rows 3 and 4 two times more. At end of Row 8—32 sts.
Row 9 Sk first hdc, sc in next st; dc in each sc and sc in each dc across to turning ch; hdc in 2nd ch of turning ch-2. Ch 2, turn.

For Size XL Only

Rows 5–8 Repeat Rows 3 and 4 two times more. At end of Row 8—33 sts.
Row 9 Repeat Row 7 for size S (see above).

For All Sizes

Row 8 (9, 10, 10) Sk first hdc; sc in each dc and dc in each sc across to turning ch; hdc in 2nd ch of turning ch-2. Ch 2, turn. Repeat Row 8 (9, 10, 10) until piece measures approx 29½ (30, 30½, 31)"/75 (76, 77.5, 79)cm from beginning, ending by working a right side row.

Neckline Shaping

Row 1 (wrong side) Sl st in first 13 sts, ch 2 (counts as hdc); sc in each dc and dc in each sc across to turning ch; hdc in 2nd ch of turning ch-2—19 (19, 20, 21) sts. Ch 2, turn.

Row 2 Sk first hdc; sc in each dc and dc in each sc across to last 4 sts (including beg ch-2)—15 (15, 16, 17) sts. Turn, leaving rem sts unworked.

Row 3 Sl st in first 5 sts, ch 2; sc in each dc and dc in each sc across to turning ch; hdc in 2nd ch of turning ch-2—11 (11, 12, 13) sts. Ch 2, turn.

Row 4 Sk first hdc; sc in each dc and dc in each sc across to last 3 sts (including beginning ch-2); hdc2tog, hdc in 2nd ch of beginning ch-2—10 (10, 11, 12) sts. Ch 2, turn.

Row 5 Sk first hdc, hdc2tog; sc in each dc and dc in each sc across to turning ch; hdc in 2nd ch of turning ch-2—9 (9, 10, 11) sts. Ch 2, turn.

Row 6 Sk first hdc, sc in each dc and dc in each sc across to turning ch; hdc in 2nd ch of turning ch-2. Ch 2, turn. Repeat Row 6, if necessary, until piece measures same as back to shoulders. Fasten off.

RIGHT FRONT

Work same as Left Front. Row 1 of Right Front is wrong side, which will result in reverse shaping.

SLEEVES

Starting at bottom, ch 31.

Row 1 (right side) Sc in 3rd ch from hook (2 skipped chs count as hdc); *dc in next ch, sc in next ch; repeat from * across to last 2 chs; dc in next ch, hdc in last ch—30 sts. Ch 2, turn.

Row 2 Sk first hdc; *sc in next dc, dc in next sc; repeat from * across to skipped chs; hdc in first skipped ch. Ch 2, turn.

Row 3 Sk first hdc; *sc in next dc, dc in next sc; repeat from * across to turning ch; hdc in 2nd ch of turning ch-2. Ch 2, turn.

Row 4 Hdc in first st; sc in each dc and dc in each sc across to turning ch; 2 hdc in 2nd ch of turning ch-2—32 sts. Ch 2, turn.

Rows 5–7 Sk first hdc, dc in next st; *sc in next dc, dc in next sc; repeat from * across to last 2 sts (including turning ch); sc in next st, hdc in 2nd ch of turning ch-2. Ch 2, turn.

Row 8 Repeat Row 4—34 sts. Ch 2, turn.

Rows 9–11 Sk first hdc, sc in next st; *dc in next sc, sc in next dc; repeat from * across to last 2 sts (including turning ch); dc in next st, hdc in 2nd ch of turning ch-2. Ch 2, turn.

Rows 12–15 Repeat Rows 4–7—36 sts.

For Sizes S and M Only

Rows 16 and 17 Repeat Row 5 two times more.

Rows 18–21 Repeat Rows 8–11—38 sts.

Rows 22–23 Repeat Row 9 two times more.

Rows 24–42 Repeat Rows 12–23 once, then repeat Rows 12–18 once more. At end of Row 42—46 sts. Repeat Row 9 until piece measures approx 18"/45.5cm from beginning, ending by working a wrong side row. At end of last row, do not ch 2. Turn.

For Sizes L and XL Only

Rows 16–19 Repeat Rows 8–11—38 sts.

Rows 20–23 Repeat Rows 4–7—40 sts.

Rows 24–27 Repeat Rows 8–11—42 sts.

Rows 28 and 29 Repeat Row 9 two times more.

Rows 30–33 Repeat Rows 4–7—44 sts.

Rows 34 and 35 Repeat Row 5 two times more.

Rows 36–41 Repeat Rows 24–29—46 sts.

Row 42 Repeat Row 4—48 sts. Repeat Row 5 until piece measures approx 18"/45.5cm from beginning, ending by working a wrong side row. At end of last row, do not ch 2. Turn.

Sleeve Cap Shaping

Row 1 (right side) Sl st in first 4 (5, 5, 6) sts, ch 2 (counts as hdc); sc in each dc and dc in each sc across to last 3 (4, 4, 5) sts (including turning ch)—40 (38, 40, 38) sts. Ch 2, turn, leaving rem sts unworked.

Row 2 Sk first st, hdc2tog; sc in each dc and dc in each sc across to last 3 sts (including beginning ch-2); hdc2tog, hdc in 2nd ch of beginning ch-2—38 (36, 38, 36) sts. Ch 2, turn.

Row 3 Sk first st, hdc2tog; sc in each dc and dc in each sc across to last 3 sts (including turning ch); hdc2tog, hdc in 2nd ch of turning ch-2—36 (34, 36, 34) sts. Ch 2, turn.

Rows 4–6 (9, 8, 11) Repeat Row 3 three (6, 5, 8) times more—30 (22, 26, 18) sts.

For Sizes S, M and L Only

Row 7 (10, 9) Sk first st, hdc2tog twice; sc in each dc and dc in each sc across to last 5 sts (including turning ch); hdc2tog twice, hdc in 2nd ch of turning ch-2—26 (18, 22) sts. Ch 2, turn.

For Size S Only

Rows 8 and 9 Repeat last row two times more—18 sts.

For Size L Only

Row 10 Repeat last row once more—18 sts.

For All Sizes

At end of last row, do not ch 2. Turn.

Row 10 (11, 11, 12) Sl st in first 4 sts, ch 2 (counts as hdc); sc in each dc and dc in each sc across to last 3 sts (including turning ch)—12 sts. Turn.

Row 11 (12, 12, 13) Repeat last row once more—6 sts. Fasten off.

FINISHING

Sew shoulder seams with 9 (9, 10, 11) sts together on each side of neck.

COLLAR

Row 1 With right side facing, join with sc in st 4"/10cm from right front center edge, work 61 more sc evenly along neckline, ending in st 4"/10cm from left front center edge—62 sc. Ch 2, turn.

Row 2 Sk first sc; *sc in next sc, dc in next sc; repeat from * across to last sc; hdc in last sc—62 sts. Ch 2, turn.

Rows 3 and 4 Sk first hdc; sc in each dc and dc in each sc across to turning ch; hdc in 2nd ch of turning ch-2. Ch 2, turn.

Row 5 Hdc in first hdc; sc in each dc and dc in each sc across to turning ch; 2 hdc in 2nd ch of turning ch-2—64 sts. Ch 2, turn.

Row 6 Sk first hdc, dc in next st; sc in each dc and dc in each sc across to last 2 sts (including turning ch); sc in next st, hdc in 2nd ch of turning ch-2. Ch 2, turn.

Rows 7 and 8 Repeat Row 3 two times more.

Row 9 Repeat Row 5—66 sts.

Row 10 Sk first hdc, sc in next st; sc in each dc and dc in each sc across to last 2 sts (including turning ch); dc in next st, hdc in 2nd ch of turning ch-2. Ch 2, turn.

Rows 11–13 Repeat Rows 5 and 6 once, then repeat Row 5 once more. At end of Row 13—70 sts.

Row 14 Repeat Row 10.
Repeat Row 3, if necessary, until collar measures approx 4½"/11.5cm from beginning. At end of last row, do not ch 2. Fasten off.

BELT
Ch 7.

Row 1 Sc in 3rd ch from hook (2 skipped chs count as hdc), dc in next ch, sc in next ch, dc in next ch, hdc in last ch—6 sts. Ch 2 (counts as first hdc on next row now and throughout), turn.

Row 2 Sk first hdc; (sc in next dc, dc in next sc) 2 times; hdc in first skipped ch. Ch 2, turn.

Row 3 Sk first hdc; (sc in next dc, dc in next sc) 2 times; hdc in 2nd ch of turning ch-2. Ch 2, turn.
Repeat Row 3 until piece measures approx 65"/165cm from beginning, or to desired length. At end of last row, do not ch 2. Fasten off.

FINISHING
Set in sleeves. Sew side and sleeve seams.

LOWER EDGING
With right side facing, work 1 row sc evenly along bottom edge of sweater.

SLEEVE EDGING
With right side facing, work 1 row sc evenly along bottom edge of sleeves.

COLLAR EDGING
With right side facing, work 1 row sc evenly along last row of collar. ◼

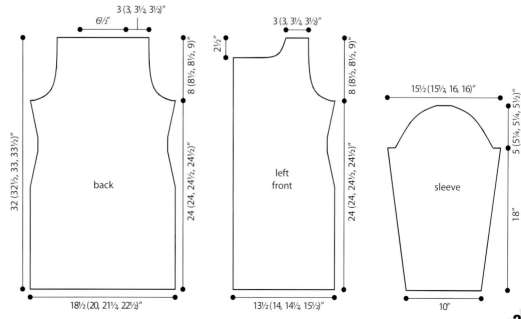

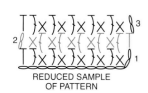

REDUCED SAMPLE
OF PATTERN

Lacy Jacket

MATERIALS

Yarn

RED HEART® *With Love*™,
7oz/198g skeins, each approx
370yds/338m (acrylic)
- 3 (4, 5) skeins #101 Eggshell

Hook

- Size H/8 (5mm) crochet hook *or size to obtain gauge*

Notions

- Stitch markers
- Yarn needle

STITCH GLOSSARY

shell Work (2 dc, ch 1, 2 dc) in st or sp indicated.

dc2tog (double crochet 2 stitches together) [Yarn over, insert hook in next st, yarn over and draw up a loop, yarn over and draw through 2 loops on hook] twice, yarn over and draw through all 3 loops on hook.

dc4tog over 2 shells [Yarn over, insert hook in ch-sp of first shell, yarn over and draw up a loop, yarn over and draw through 2 loops on hook] twice (3 loops on hook), [yarn over, insert hook in ch-sp of last shell, yarn over and draw up a loop, yarn over and draw through 2 loops on hook] twice (5 loops on hook), yarn over and draw through all 5 loops on hook.

SIZES

S/M (L/1X, 2X/3X)

FINISHED MEASUREMENTS

Bust 38 (46, 54)"/96.5 (117, 137)cm
Length 18 (19½, 21)"/45.5 (49.5, 53.5)cm, including edging

GAUGE

6 ch-3 sps and 2 shell borders = 6"/15cm;
7 shell rows = 4"/10cm, slightly stretched and worked on the bias (diagonally); 4 ch-3 sps = 3¾"/9.5cm, slightly stretched and worked horizontally.
Remember to check gauge for best results!

NOTES

1 Cardigan is worked in five pieces; left panel, right panel, back, and two side gussets.
2 Four different pattern stitches are worked within a border of shell stitches throughout. After the first shell and before the last shell, an increase or decrease may be worked. The appropriate pattern stitch is worked between the shell borders and any increases or decreases. All rows of left panel, right panel, and back are of the following form: shell, increase/decrease/even, work in pattern stitch across, increase/decrease/even, shell.
3 Because of increasing and decreasing on the edges, the final repeat of any pattern stitch may not be worked to completion. Only continue working the stitch repeats until you reach the last ch-sp before the shell border.

PATTERN STITCHES

Shell Border at Beginning and End of Rows

Row 1 Ch 3, turn, shell in ch-sp of first shell, ch 2; work in established pattern stitch across and into last ch-sp before last shell, ch 2, shell in ch-sp of last shell, dc in 3rd ch of turning ch-3.

Row 2 Ch 3, turn, shell in ch-sp of first shell, ch 3, sk next ch-sp; work in established pattern stitch across to last ch-sp before last shell (do not work in last ch-sp); ch 3, sk last ch-sp, shell in ch-sp of last shell, dc in 3rd ch of turning ch-3.
Repeat Rows 1 and 2 for Shell Border pattern (worked even, without incs or decs).

Shaping Inside Shell Border Pattern

Increase inside Shell Border at Beginning of Row Ch 3, turn, shell in ch-sp of first shell, ch 3; work in established pattern stitches across, working first st in next ch-sp.

Increase inside Shell Border at End of Row Work in established pattern stitches across and into last ch-sp before last shell; ch 3, shell in ch-sp of last shell, dc in 3rd ch of turning ch-3.

Decrease inside Shell Border at Beginning of Row Ch 3, turn, shell in ch-sp of first shell, ch 3, sk next ch-sp; work in established pattern stitches across.

Decrease inside Shell Border at End of Row Work in established pattern stitches across to last ch-sp before last shell (do not work in last ch-sp); ch 3, sk last ch-sp, shell in ch-sp of last shell, dc in 3rd ch of turning ch-3.

Chain Mesh

Row 1 Sc in next ch-sp; *ch 3, sc in next ch-sp; repeat from * across to shell border.
Repeat Row 1 for Chain Mesh pattern.

Flower Mesh

Note Markers are used to indicate placement of each flower. Markers are removed in Row 1 as each flower is started. New markers are placed in Row 4 for next repeat.

Row 1 Sc in next ch-sp; *[ch 3, sc in next ch-sp] across to next marked sc, 3 dc in marked sc between ch-sps, sc in next ch-sp; repeat from * over all marked sc, end with [ch 3, sc in next ch-sp] across to shell border. Remove all markers.

Row 2 Sc in next ch-sp; *[ch 3, sc in next ch-sp] across to next 3-dc group, 2 dc in each of next 3 dc, sc in next ch-sp; repeat from * over all 3-dc groups, end with [ch 3, sc in next ch-sp] across to shell border.

Row 3 Sc in next ch-sp; *[ch 3, sc in next ch-sp] across to next dc, ch 2, [dc2tog in next 2 dc, ch 2] 3 times, sc in next ch-sp; repeat from * over all 6-dc groups, end with [ch 3, sc in next ch-sp] across to shell border.

Row 4 Sc in next ch-sp; *[ch 3, sc in next ch-sp] across to next ch-2 sp, place marker in last sc made, sk next ch-2 sp, [ch 3, sc in next dc2tog] 3 times, ch 3, sk next ch-2 sp, sc in next ch-sp, place marker in last sc made; repeat from * over all dc2tog, end with [ch 3, sc in next ch-sp] across to shell border.
Repeat Rows 1–4 for Flower Mesh pattern.

Box-in-Diamond

Row 1 Sc in next ch-sp; *ch 3, 3 dc in next ch-sp ('box' made), ch 3, sc in next ch-sp; repeat from * across to shell border.

Row 2 Sc in next ch-sp; *ch 3, sc in next ch-sp; repeat from * across to shell border.

Row 3 Sc in next ch-sp, [ch 3, sc in next ch-sp] across to first ch-sp centered between and above 2 boxes 2 rows below; *ch 3, 3 dc in next ch-sp, ch 3, sc in next ch-sp; repeat from * across to shell border, working extra [ch 3, sc in next ch-sp] as needed before shell border.

Row 4 Repeat Row 2.

Rows 5 and 6 Repeat Rows 1 and 2.

Zig-Zag Mesh

Row 1 Sc in next ch-sp; *3 dc in next sc between ch-sps, sc in next ch-sp, ch 3, sc in next ch-sp; repeat from * across to shell border.

Row 2 Sc in next ch-sp; *3 dc in next sc, sc in next ch-sp or center dc of next 3-dc group; repeat from * across to shell border.

Row 3 Sc in next ch-sp, [ch 3, sc in center dc of next 3-dc group] across to first sc centered above a ch-sp 2 rows below (not an sc centered above a 3-dc group); *3 dc in next sc, sc in center dc of next 3-dc group, ch 3, sc in center dc of next 3-dc group; repeat from * across to shell border.

Row 4 Sc in next ch-sp; *ch 3, sc in next ch-sp or center dc of next 3-dc group; repeat from * across to shell border.

Lace and Ladder

Row 1 Sc in next ch-sp, ch 1, dc in next sc; ch 1, sc in next ch-sp, *ch 1, dc in next sc, ch 1, sc in next ch-sp; repeat from * across to shell border.

Row 2 Sk first ch-1 sp, sc in next dc; *ch 1, sk next ch-1 sp; if next st is a sc, work dc in sc; if next st is a dc, work sc in dc; repeat from * across to shell border, ending with sk last ch-1 sp.

Row 3 Sc in next ch-sp, ch 1, dc in next sc; *ch 1, sk next ch-1 sp, dc in next st; repeat from * across to shell border, ending with ch 1, sc in last ch-sp.

Row 4 Sk first ch-1 sp, dc in next dc; *ch 1, sc in next dc, ch 1, dc in next dc; repeat from * across to shell border, ending with sk last ch-1 sp.

Row 5 Sc in next ch-sp, ch 1, sc in next dc; *ch 1, sk next ch-1 sp; if next st is a sc, work dc in sc; if next st is a dc, work sc in dc; repeat from * across to shell border, ending with ch 1, sc in last ch-sp.

PATTERN STITCH SEQUENCE

Work shell border on both edges of each row and work the following pattern stitches between the borders, increasing and decreasing inside the shell border as instructed, **work 3 repeats of Flower Mesh, *work 1 row in Chain Mesh, work Box-in-Diamond, work 1 row in Chain Mesh, work Zig-Zag Mesh, work 1 row in Chain Mesh, work Lace and Ladder, work 2 rows in Chain Mesh; repeat from ** as needed.

LEFT PANEL

Note Left panel is worked on the bias (diagonally) from lower front corner (at side edge), up to armhole where sleeve is joined, then up and over shoulder, and down to lower back edge.

Left Front

Row 1 (wrong side) Ch 3, shell in 3rd ch from hook.

Row 2 Ch 3, turn; (2 dc, ch 1, 2 dc, ch 1, 2 dc) in ch-1 sp, dc in 3rd ch of beginning ch-3.

Row 3 Ch 3, turn; shell in first ch-1 sp, ch 1, shell in last ch-1 sp, dc in 3rd ch of turning ch-3.

Row 4 Ch 3, turn; shell in ch-sp of first shell, ch 3, sc in next ch-1 sp, ch 3, shell in ch-sp of last shell, dc in 3rd ch of turning ch-3.

Row 5 Ch 3, turn; shell in ch-sp of first shell, ch 3, sc in next ch-sp, 3 dc in next sc, sc in next ch-sp, ch 3, shell in ch-sp of last shell, dc in 3rd ch of turning ch-3.

Row 6 Ch 3, turn; shell in ch-sp of first shell, ch 3, sc in next ch-sp, 2 dc in each of next 3 dc, sc in next ch-sp, ch 3, shell in ch-sp of last shell, dc in 3rd ch of turning ch-3.

Row 7 Ch 3, turn; shell in ch-sp of first shell, ch 3, sc in next ch-sp, ch 2, [dc2tog in next 2 dc, ch 2] 3 times, sc in next ch-sp, ch 3, shell in ch-sp of last shell, dc in 3rd ch of turning ch-3.

Row 8 Ch 3, turn; shell in ch-sp of first shell, ch 3, sc in next ch-sp, sk next ch-2 sp, [ch 3, sc in next dc2tog] 3 times, ch 3, sk next ch-2 sp, sc in next ch-sp, ch 3, shell in ch-sp of last shell, dc in 3rd ch of turning ch-3.

Continue in Pattern Stitch Sequence beginning at *, inc at beginning and end of each row, until piece measures 8 (9, 10)"/20.5 (23, 25.5) cm measured along a side diagonal edge.

Use different color markers to mark front edge and side edge. Front edge is at beginning of wrong side rows; side edge is at beginning of right side rows.

Front Edge Shaping

Continue in Pattern Stitch Sequence, dec at front edge and inc at side edge of each row, until side edge measures 10 (10½, 11)"/25.5 (26.5, 28)cm, end by working a wrong side row. Fasten off. Make a note of last row worked.

Left Sleeve

Beginning at front cuff edge, work as for left front through Row 4. Place a marker in sc on Row 4 (for flower placement). Work in Pattern Stitch Sequence beginning at **, inc at beginning and end of each row until same pattern row as last row of left front is worked.

Joining Row (right side) Turn, continue in Pattern Stitch Sequence across sleeve to shell border; continue in established pattern stitch across final shell of sleeve and beginning shell of left front, as follows: treat ch-1 sp of final shell of sleeve as next ch-sp or st, then continue in established pattern stitch and join sleeve and left front by inserting hook into both turning ch of sleeve and last dc worked on last row of left front to work next st, treat ch-1 sp of first shell of left front as next ch-sp or st; continue in established pattern stitch across left front, working shell border at end of row. Move side edge marker to cuff edge. Cuff edge is at beginning of right side rows. Continue in Pattern Stitch Sequence across combined left front and left sleeve piece, dec at front edge and inc at cuff edge of each row, until cuff edge measures 15 (17, 19)"/38 (43, 48.5)cm.

Back Sleeve Edge Shaping

Continue in Pattern Stitch Sequence, dec at beginning and end of each row until front edge measures 13½ (15, 16½)"/34.5 (38, 42)cm, ending by working a wrong side row. Move cuff edge marker to back sleeve edge. Back sleeve edge is at beginning of right side rows.

Neck Shaping

Measure 3"/7.5cm straight across from front edge. Place a marker in working row directly above this point, in a ch-sp or centered above a ch-sp in previous row. Keep the marker in place to indicate beginning of neck shaping (you will need this when working the right panel).
Dec at beginning of next row and continue in Pattern Stitch Sequence across to marker, ch 3, shell in marked st or sp; leave remaining sts unworked.

Continue in Pattern Stitch Sequence, dec at beginning and end of each row until back sleeve edge measures the same as front sleeve edge.

Back Side Edge Shaping

Continue in Pattern Stitch Sequence, dec at front edge and inc at side edge of each row, until back side edge measures about ½"/1.5cm less than front side edge.

Lower Back Edge Shaping

Continue in Pattern Stitch Sequence, dec at both edges of each row, until only 3 ch-sps remain between border shells.
Note Discontinue pattern stitches and work only in Chain Mesh when there is no longer sufficient space to reasonably work patterns.

Last 3 Rows

Next Row Ch 3, turn; shell in ch-sp of first shell, ch 2, sk next ch-sp, sc in next ch-sp, ch 2, sk next ch-sp, shell in ch-sp of last shell, dc in 3rd ch of turning ch-3.
Next to Last Row Ch 3, turn; 2 dc in ch-sp of first shell, ch 1, dc4tog in ch-sps of first and last shells, ch 1, 2 dc in ch-sp of last shell, dc in 3rd ch of turning ch-3.
Last Row Ch 3, turn; dc4tog in ch-sps of first and last shells, dc in 3rd ch of turning ch-3. Fasten off.

Complete Neck Edge

Row 1 With right side facing, join yarn with sl st in first dc of unworked shell at lower edge of neck shaping (last row worked before neck shaping), ch 3, shell in ch-sp of shell, dc in 3rd ch of turning ch.
Row 2 Ch 3, turn; shell in ch-sp of shell, dc in 3rd ch of beginning/turning ch-3.
Repeat Row 2 until piece is long enough to lie smoothly along section of neck edge without border shells (approx 5 rows total). Fasten off, leaving a long tail. Use long tail to sew border to neck edge.

RIGHT PANEL NOTES

1 Right panel is worked back and forth (horizontally) from lower front edge up to armhole where sleeve is shaped, then up and over shoulder, and down to lower back edge.
2 Gently stretch panel throughout before measuring.

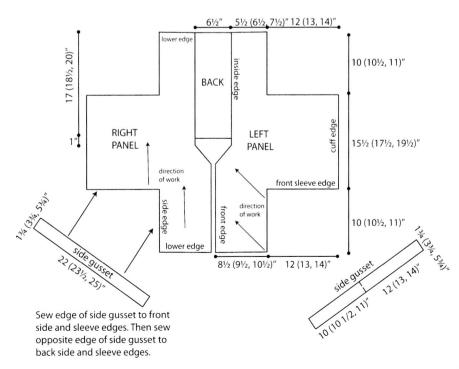

Sew edge of side gusset to front side and sleeve edges. Then sew opposite edge of side gusset to back side and sleeve edges.

Right Front

Ch 31 (36, 41).

Row 1 (right side) Sc in 2nd ch from hook, sc in next ch; *ch 1, sk next ch, sc in next 4 chs; repeat from * across to last 3 chs; ch 1, sk next ch, sc in last 2 chs—24 (28, 32) sc and 6 (7, 8) ch-1 sps.

Row 2 Ch 3, turn; shell in each ch-1 sp across, dc in last sc—6 (7, 8) shells.

Row 3 Ch 3, turn; shell in ch-sp of first shell, ch 2; *sc in next sp between shells**; ch 3, sc in next ch-1 sp, ch 3; repeat from * across to last shell, ending last repeat at **; ch 2, shell in ch-sp of last shell, dc in 3rd ch of turning ch-3. Place a marker in 3rd and 7th (3rd and 7th; 3rd, 7th and 11th) sc (for flower placement in Flower Mesh pattern).

Work in Pattern Stitch Sequence beginning at **, with no increasing or decreasing (begin with Row 2 of Shell Border), until side measures ½"/1.5cm less than left front side edge; end by working a right side row. Do not fasten off.

Right Sleeve Front Edge Shaping

Row 1 (wrong side) Ch 46 (51, 56), turn; 2 dc in 5th ch from hook, ch 1, 2 dc in next ch, [sk next 3 chs, 2 dc in next ch, ch 1, 2 dc in next ch] 8 (9, 10) times, ch 3, sc in ch-1 sp of border shell, ch 3, sc in next ch-2 sp, continue in established pattern stitch across.

Continue in Pattern Stitch Sequence, with no increasing or decreasing, until front edge measures ½"/1.5cm longer than left front side edge to beginning of neck shaping. End by working a right side row.

Neck Shaping

Continue in Pattern Stitch Sequence, dec at neck edge of next 4 rows.

Continue in Pattern Stitch Sequence, with no increasing or decreasing, until cuff edge measures about 1½"/4cm less that left cuff edge; end by working a right side row.

Right Sleeve Back Edge Shaping

Row 1 (wrong side) Ch 3, turn; shell in ch-sp of first shell, shell in next sc; *sk next sc, shell in next sc; repeat from * across to approx 5 (6, 7)"/12.5 (15, 18)cm before inside edge (opposite cuff edge); treating last shell worked as border shell, continue in established pattern stitch across.

Continue in Pattern Stitch Sequence, with no increasing or decreasing, until side edge measures same as front side edge.

Lower Back Edge Shaping

Next Row Ch 3, turn; shell in ch-sp of first shell; *sk next st, shell in next st; repeat from * across to last shell; shell in ch-sp of last shell, dc in 3rd ch of turning ch.

Last Row Ch 1, turn; sl st in each st across to ch-sp of first shell, ch 1, sc in same ch-sp; *shell in sp between shells, sc in ch-sp of next shell; repeat from * across. Fasten off.

Lower Front Edge Shaping

Row 1 With right side facing, and working along opposite side of foundation ch, join yarn with sl st in ch at base of first sc; ch 3, shell in each ch-1 sp across, dc in ch at base of last sc.

Row 2 Repeat last row of Lower Back Edge Shaping.

BACK

Rows 1–7 Beginning at lower back edge, work same as Rows 1–7 on Left Front.

Row 8 Ch 3, turn; shell in ch-sp of first shell, ch 3, sc in next ch-sp, place a marker in sc just made (for flower placement), sk next ch-2 sp, [ch 3, sc in next dc2tog] 3 times, ch 3, sk next ch-2 sp, sc in next ch-sp, place a marker in sc just made, ch 3, shell in ch-sp of last shell, dc in 3rd ch of turning ch-3.

Work 2 more repeats of Flower Mesh. Work in Pattern Stitch Sequence beginning at *, inc at beginning and end of each row until piece measures 6"/15cm measured along a side edge.

Continue in Pattern Stitch Sequence, inc at beginning and dec at end of each row until longest edge measures 16½ (18, 19½)"/42 (45.5, 49.5)cm.

Lower Back Edge Shaping

Continue in Pattern Stitch Sequence, dec at both edges of each row, until only 3 ch-sps remain between border shells.

Note Discontinue pattern stitches and work only in Chain Mesh when there is no longer sufficient space to reasonably work patterns.

Next Row, Next to Last Row and Last Row Work same as last 3 rows on Left Panel.

SIDE GUSSETS (MAKE 2)

Ch 8 (14, 20).

Row 1 Sc in 2nd ch from hook; *ch 3, sk next 2 chs, sc in next ch; repeat from * across—2 (4, 6) ch-3 sps.

Row 2 Ch 5 (counts as dc and ch-2 sp), turn; sc in next ch-3 sp; *ch 3, sc in next ch-3 sp; repeat from * across to last sc; ch 2, dc in last sc—2 dc, 2 ch-2 sps and 1 (3, 5) ch-3 sps.

Row 3 Ch 1, turn; sc in first dc, *ch 3, sc in next ch-3 sp; repeat from * across to turning ch; ch 3, sc in 3rd ch of turning ch-5—2 (4, 6) ch-3 sps.

Repeat Rows 2 and 3 until piece measures 22 (23½, 25)"/56 (59.5, 63.5)cm from beginning. Fasten off.

Lacy Jacket

Note Gently stretch fabric width-wise to about 1¾ (3¾, 5¾)"/4.5 (9.5, 14.5)cm wide, before measuring.

Blocking and Seaming
Block each piece to schematic measurements. Arrange pieces according to assembly diagram. With right sides tog, whip stitch edges to join.

Edging
Note Different angles at which stitch patterns are worked on left and right panel cause fabric to stretch differently. As a result, neck and front edges of left and right front may differ slightly. To help even length and shape of front and neck edges, you may wish to skip more sts when working sc along one front edge, and skip fewer sts when working sc along opposite front edge. Similarly, you may wish to work decs on one side of back neck and incs on opposite side of back neck.
Round 1 With right side facing, join yarn with sl st in edge of row 1 at lower front corner of right panel; work sc evenly along front edge, across neck edge and down opposite front edge; ch 2, working along lower edge, work shell in edge of every other row along lower edges of left panel and back, in ch-sp of each shell along lower edges of right panel and in each sc (or in ch at base of each sc) along lower edge of each gusset across to beginning.
Round 2 Ch 2, sc evenly along front edge, across neck edge and down opposite front edge, shell in ch-sp of each shell across lower edge, ch 1; join with sl st in first sc. Fasten off. Weave in all ends. ■

REDUCED SAMPLE OF CHAIN MESH PATTERN
WITH SHELL BORDER AT ENDS OF ROWS

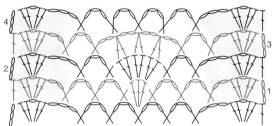

REDUCED SAMPLE OF FLOWER MESH PATTERN
WITH SHELL BORDER AT ENDS OF ROWS

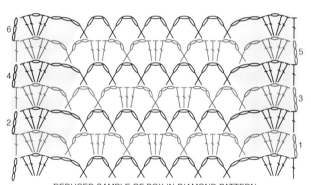

REDUCED SAMPLE OF BOX-IN-DIAMOND PATTERN
WITH SHELL BORDER AT ENDS OF ROWS

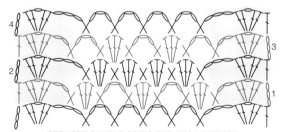

REDUCED SAMPLE OF ZIG ZAG MESH PATTERN
WITH SHELL BORDER AT ENDS OF ROWS

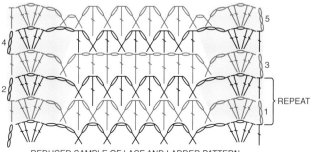

REDUCED SAMPLE OF LACE AND LADDER PATTERN
WITH SHELL BORDER AT ENDS OF ROWS

Perfect Fit Blazer

MATERIALS

Yarn

RED HEART® *Soft Yarn*, 5oz/141g skeins, each approx 256yds/234m (acrylic)
• 5 (6, 7, 7, 8) skeins #4600 White

Hook
• Size I/9 (5.5mm) crochet hook *or size to obtain gauge*

Notions
• 7 buttons, 1¼"/30mm diameter
• Stitch markers
• Yarn needle

STITCH GLOSSARY

sc2tog (sc 2 sts together) [Insert hook in next st, yo and draw up a loop] twice, yo and draw through all 3 loops on hook.

SIZES
S (M, L, 1X, 2X)

FINISHED MEASUREMENTS
Chest 32 (36, 40, 44½, 48)"/81.5 (91.5, 101.5, 113, 122)cm
Length 20 (21, 21, 22½, 22 ½)"/51 (53.5, 53.5, 57, 57)cm

NOTE
Jacket has a little stretch and is designed to be close-fitting.

GAUGE
15 sc and 18 rows = 4"/10cm using size I/9 (5.5mm) crochet hook.
Remember to check gauge for best results!

BACK
Ch 65 (73, 81, 89, 95).
Row 1 Sc in 2nd ch from hook and each ch across—64 (72, 80, 88, 94) sc.
Row 2 Ch 1, turn, sc in each st across.
Row 3 (dec row) Ch 1, turn, sc in first 23 sc, sc2tog, place marker in sc2tog, sc in next 14 (22, 30, 38, 44) sc, sc2tog, place marker in sc2tog, sc in last 23 sc—62 (70, 78, 86, 92) sts.
Rows 4 and 5 Repeat Row 2.
Row 6 (dec row) Ch 1, turn, sc in each sc to marker, sc2tog, sc in each sc to one sc before marker, sc2tog, sc in each sc across—60 (68, 76, 84, 90) sts.
Rows 7–27 Repeat last 3 rows 7 more times—46 (54, 62, 70, 76) sts.
Row 28 Ch 1, turn, sc in each st across. Repeat last row until back measures 7½ (7½, 7½, 8, 8)"/19 (19, 19, 20.5, 20.5)cm from beginning.
Next Row (inc row) Ch 1, turn, sc in first sc, 2 sc in next sc, sc in each sc across to last 2 sc, 2 sc in next sc, sc in last sc—48 (56, 64, 72, 78) sts.
Next 2 Rows Ch 1, turn, sc in each sc across.
Repeat last 3 rows 6 more times—60 (68, 76, 84, 90) sts.
Next Row Ch 1, turn, sc in each sc across. Repeat last row until back measures 12½ (12½, 12½, 13, 13)"/32 (32, 32, 33, 33)cm from beginning.

Shape Armholes
Row 1 Ch 1, turn, sl st in first 3 sts, ch 1, sc in next 2 sts, sc2tog, sc in each st across to last 7 sts, sc2tog, sc in next 2 sts; leave rem 3 sts unworked—52 (60, 68, 76, 82) sts.
Rows 2 and 3 (dec row) Ch 1, turn, sc in first 2 sts, sc2tog, sc in each st across to last 4 sts, sc2tog, sc in last 2 sts—48 (56, 64, 72, 78) sts.
Row 4 Ch 1, turn, sc in each st across. Repeat last row until armhole measures 7½ (8½, 8½, 9½, 9½)"/19 (21.5, 21.5, 24, 24)cm.

Shape Shoulders
Row 1 Ch 1, turn, sl st in first 2 sts, ch 1, sc in next 3 (4, 5, 5, 6) sts, hdc in next 3 (4, 5, 5, 6) sts, dc in next 3 (4, 5, 5, 6) sts, tr in next 3 (3, 4, 6, 6) sts, fasten off, sk center 20 (22, 22, 26, 26) sts and rejoin yarn in next st, ch 4 (counts as tr), tr in next 2 (2, 3, 5, 5) sts, dc in next 3 (4, 5, 5, 6) sts, hdc in next 3 (4, 5, 5, 6) sts, sc in next 3 (4, 5, 5, 6) sts; leave last 2 sts unworked. Fasten off.

LEFT FRONT
Ch 22 (24, 27, 29, 31).
Row 1 (right side) Sc in 2nd ch from hook and each ch across—21 (23, 26, 28, 30) sc.
Row 2 Ch 1, turn, sc in first st, 2 sc in next st, sc in each st across—22 (24, 27, 29, 31) sc.
Row 3 Ch 1, turn, sc in first st, sc2tog, sc in each st across to last 2 sts, 2 sc in next st, sc in last st.
Continue to inc 1 st in this way at front edge every row 13 more times, AT THE SAME TIME, dec 1 st at armhole edge every 4th row 6 more times—29 (31, 34, 36, 38) sts.
Next Row Ch 1, turn, sc in each st across. Repeat last row until front measures 7½ (7½, 7½, 8, 8)"/19 (19, 19, 20.5, 20.5)cm from beginning.
Inc 1 st at armhole edge on next row then every 3rd row 6 more times—36 (38, 41, 43, 45) sts, AT THE SAME TIME, when front measures 10½ (10½, 10½, 11, 11)"/26.5 (26.5, 26.5, 28, 28)cm from beginning, shape lapel as follows.

Shape Lapel
Inc 1 st in 3rd st from front edge on next row, then every 6th row 3 more times. When front measures same as back to armhole, shape armhole as on back.
Next Row Ch 1, turn, sc in each st across—34 (36, 39, 41, 43) sts.
Repeat last row until armhole measures 5½ (5½, 5½, 6, 6)"/14 (14, 14, 15, 15)cm, end with a right side row.
Next Row (wrong side) Ch 1, turn, sl st in first 12 sts (for lapel), sc2tog, sc in each st across—21 (23, 26, 28, 30) sts.
Continue to dec 1 st at lapel edge every row 7 (6, 5, 5, 4) more times—14 (17, 21, 23, 26) sts. When armhole measures same as back, shape shoulder as for back.

RIGHT FRONT
Work as for left front, reversing all shaping and working 3 buttonholes evenly spaced along front edge. Work buttonholes, beginning at front edge, as follows: Sc in first 2 sts, ch 1, sk 1 st, complete row as established.

RIGHT SLEEVE

Left Side

Ch 25 (27, 29, 31, 33).

Row 1 Sc in 2nd ch from hook and in each ch across—24 (26, 28, 30, 32) sc.

Rows 2–15 Ch 1, turn, sc in each sc across. Fasten off.

Right Side

Ch 15 (17, 19, 21, 23).

Row 1 Sc in 2nd ch from hook and each ch across—14 (16, 18, 20, 22) sc.

Rows 2–15 Ch 1, turn, sc in each sc across. Do not fasten off.

Join Right and Left Sides

Row 1 (right side) Ch 1, turn, sc in first 13 (15, 17, 19, 21) sc of right side; place first st of left side on top of last st of right side and work and sc through both sts, sc in next 23 (25, 27, 29, 31) sc of left side—37 (41, 45, 49, 53) sts.

Row 2 Ch 1, turn, sc in first st, 2 sc in next st, sc across to last 2 sts, 2 sc in next st, sc in last st—39 (43, 47, 51, 55) sts.

Rows 3–8 Ch 1, turn, sc in each sc across.

Rows 9–29 Repeat Rows 2–8—45 (49, 53, 57, 61) sts.

Repeat Row 3 until sleeve measures 12½ (12½, 13, 13, 13½)"/32 (32, 33, 33, 34.5) cm from beginning.

Shape Cap

Row 1 Ch 1, turn, sl st in first 3 sts, ch 1, sc in next st, sc2tog, sc in each st across to last 6 sts, sc2tog, sc in next st; leave rem 3 sts unworked—37 (41, 45, 49, 53) sts.

Row 2 Ch 1, turn, sc in first st, sc2tog, sc in each st across to last 3 sts, sc2tog, sc in last st—35 (39, 43, 47, 51) sts.

Row 3 Ch 1, turn, sc in each st across.

Rows 4–13 Repeat Rows 2 and 3—25 (29, 33, 37, 41) sts.

Rows 14–21 Ch 1, turn, sc in each st across.

Rows 22–25 Repeat Row 2—17 (21, 25, 29, 33) sts. Fasten off.

LEFT SLEEVE

Work as for right sleeve, reversing right side and left side and joining by overlapping sides in reverse.

David Lazarus

Perfect Fit Blazer

FINISHING

Sew shoulder seams.

Collar

Place stitch markers in the 6th st from each front edge of lapel (lapel markers). Place stitch markers 3½"/9cm in from the lapel markers (neck markers). From the wrong side, join yarn in the first neck marker, ch 1, work 48 (54, 60, 68, 72) sc evenly spaced across to the second neck marker.

Next Row Ch 1, sc in next st, 2 sc in next st, sc in each st across to last 2 sts, 2 sc in next st, sc in next st.

Repeat last row 11 more times. Place stitch markers on each end of last row (collar markers).

Next 7 Rows Ch 1, turn, sc in each st across—72 (78, 84, 92, 96) sc. Fasten off. From the wrong side, sew edges of lapels to edges of collar, aligning lapel and collar markers.

Sew side and sleeve seams. Set in sleeves.

Trim

From right side, join yarn in lower edge at a side seam.

Round 1 (right side) Ch 1, work sc evenly spaced all the way around jacket; join with sl st in first sc.

Round 2 (wrong side) Turn, sl st in each sc around. Fasten off.

Sleeve Trim

From right side, join yarn in top of overlapping sleeve sides.

Row 1 (right side) Ch 1, work sc evenly spaced down overlapping edge, around end of sleeve and up other overlapping edge.

Round 2 (wrong side) Turn, sl st in each sc around. Fasten off.

Sew 3 buttons to left front corresponding with buttonholes. Sewing through both thicknesses, sew 2 buttons on each cuff. ■

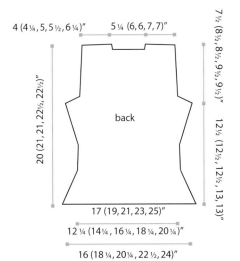

back

4 (4¼, 5, 5½, 6¼)"   5¼ (6, 6, 7, 7)"

7½ (8½, 8½, 9½, 9½)"

20 (21, 21, 22½, 22½)"

12½ (12½, 12½, 13, 13)"

17 (19, 21, 23, 25)"

12¼ (14¼, 16¼, 18¼, 20¼)"

16 (18¼, 20¼, 22½, 24)"

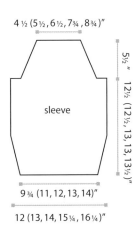

sleeve

4½ (5½, 6½, 7¾, 8¾)"

5½"

12½ (12½, 13, 13, 13½)"

9¾ (11, 12, 13, 14)"

12 (13, 14, 15¼, 16¼)"

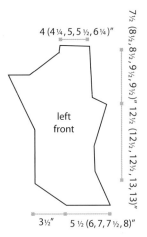

left front

4 (4¼, 5, 5½, 6¼)"

7½ (8½, 8½, 9½, 9½)"

12½ (12½, 12½, 13, 13)"

3½"   5½ (6, 7, 7½, 8)"